T0057419

Praise for *The "I Don't Want to Cook" Book*

"*The "I Don't Want to Cook" Book* is exactly the kind of cookbook we all want—without even knowing we want it. Alyssa brings her masterful touch to creating simple—yet mouthwatering—recipes that take no more than 15 minutes of prep time, like Creamy Paprika Chicken Skillet with Spinach and Tomatoes, or Red Curry Salmon with Snow Peas. And all of her tips for streamlining the cooking process are worth the price of admission alone."

—CAROLYN KETCHUM,
author of *Easy Keto Dinners* and *The Ultimate Guide to Keto Baking*

"Alyssa knew the heart of almost every home cook when she wrote *The "I Don't Want to Cook" Book*. Juggling work, family, and social life can be daunting and overwhelming. Now even when we don't *want* to cook, we can get meals made and nutrition ingested, and do it in a way that is delicious and satisfying!"

—JENNIFER LB ROBINS,
founder of Predominantly Paleo and Legit Bread Company;
bestselling author of *Down South Paleo*, *The Paleo Kids Cookbook*, *Paleo Cooking
with Your Instant Pot* ®, and *Affordable Paleo Cooking with Your Instant Pot* ®;
coauthor of *The New Yiddish Kitchen*

"If you could only purchase one cookbook, please let this be the one! We all get in cooking ruts, but this family-friendly and approachable cookbook helps you avoid it altogether."

—MELISSA ERDELAC,
author of *Frugal Gluten-Free Cooking*

"With mouthwatering, fuss-free whole-food recipes and fresh ingredient shortcuts for when you just don't want to cook, Alyssa has brilliantly given us a delicious new cookbook that doesn't compromise flavor or nutrition."

—KARISTA BENNETT,
author of *The Oregon Farm Table Cookbook*

Praise for *The "I Don't Want to Cook" Book*

"Alyssa has a knack for creating quick and effortless meals that are loaded with fresh ingredients and big flavors. Between Deconstructed Hummus Salad with Cucumber and Tomato—and Philly Cheesesteak–Stuffed Bell Pepper Halves—there is a delicious meal for everyone at the table!"

—SAMANTHA FERRARO,
author of *The Weeknight Mediterranean Kitchen*

"I've known Alyssa on the food blogging scene for years, and I *love* her cooking tips for how *not* to live in the kitchen when cooking healthy meals for busy families. And this book couldn't explain her style better. *The "I Don't Want to Cook" Book* is filled with tips on how *not* to cook, and recipes that use no-nonsense ways to cook healthy and simple meals without using processed ingredients. It begins with the basic staples you need in your pantry for those days when you don't know what to cook. Alyssa teaches you how to shop, plan, and prep your mise en place. But, more importantly, the recipes are separated in easy chapters for quick reference. She also includes different methods of cooking for those who love kitchen appliances and gadgets. I *love* this book and I know you will too!"

—DR. KAREN S. LEE,
author of *No-Thaw Paleo Cooking in Your Instant Pot®*, *Keto Cooking with*
Your Instant Pot®*, and *Paleo Cooking with Your Air Fryer

"For those days when you are struggling to find the time or energy to head to the kitchen (which is most days these days—let's be honest!), *The "I Don't Want to Cook" Book* is every mom's dream: simple ingredient lists, easy instructions, helpful tips, and whole-food recipes that don't skimp on flavor. Stop what you're doing and get this book!"

—KELLY PFEIFFER,
author of *Superfood Weeknight Meals*; creator of @eattherainbow_kids

THE "I DON'T WANT TO COOK" BOOK

100 TASTY, HEALTHY, LOW-PREP RECIPES for When You Just DON'T Want to Cook

ALYSSA BRANTLEY
FOUNDER OF EVERYDAYMAVEN

ADAMS MEDIA
New York London Toronto Sydney New Delhi

Aadamsmedia

Adams Media
An Imprint of Simon & Schuster, LLC
100 Technology Center Drive
Stoughton, Massachusetts 02072

First Adams Media hardcover edition
July 2022

ADAMS MEDIA and colophon are trademarks
of Simon & Schuster.

For information about special discounts for
bulk purchases, please contact Simon &
Schuster Special Sales at 1-866-506-1949 or
business@simonandschuster.com.

The Simon & Schuster Speakers Bureau can
bring authors to your live event. For more
information or to book an event contact the
Simon & Schuster Speakers Bureau at
1-866-248-3049 or visit our website at
www.simonspeakers.com.

Interior design, illustrations, and
hand lettering by Priscilla Yuen
Photographs by Kelly Smith
Interior images © 123RF/lekstuntkite,
kwangmoo, Oxana Lebedeva

Manufactured in the United States of America

10 9 8 7 6 5 4

Library of Congress Cataloging-in-Publication
Data
Names: Brantley, Alyssa, author.
Title: The "I don't want to cook" book /
Alyssa Brantley, Founder of EverydayMaven.
Description: First Adams Media hardcover
edition. | Stoughton, Massachusetts:
Adams Media, 2022 | Includes index.
Identifiers: LCCN 2022006124 |
ISBN 9781507219195 (hc) |
ISBN 9781507219201 (ebook)
Subjects: LCSH: Quick and easy cooking. |
LCGFT: Cookbooks.
Classification: LCC TX833.5 .B69 2022 |
DDC 641.5/12--dc23/eng/20220318
LC record available at
https://lccn.loc.gov/2022006124

ISBN 978-1-5072-1919-5
ISBN 978-1-5072-1920-1 (ebook)

For my parents and brother, who taught me to love
and explore food from as early as I can remember.
And, to my three forget-me-nots—
there is no greater love.

CoN

TENTS

LESS-WORK LUNCHES / 51

3

4

SUPER-EASY SALADS / 67

SERIOUSLY SIMPLE SOUPS / 87

5

6

SAVORY SMALL PLATES AND SIDES / 107

7 DINNERS THAT DON'T TAKE ALL DAY / 127

EFFORTLESS SWEET TREATS / 173

8

INTRO

Are you too busy to plan (let alone make!) dinner? Would you rather spend the hours of a weekend afternoon having fun or checking something off your to-do list than figuring out lunch? Do you often forget about breakfast in the morning rush?

For those days when you are struggling to find the time or energy to head to the kitchen, *The "I Don't Want to Cook" Book* is here to help! First, you'll get a crash course on how to make cooking a healthy and tasty meal as quick and easy as possible. In Chapter 1, you'll learn how to cut down on the prep work of peeling, chopping, and more by opting for precut fresh or frozen vegetables. You'll also discover the staple items you should always have on hand, like grated Parmesan and jarred sauces, so you can make meals in minutes. And for those instances when you don't have a certain ingredient, you'll explore easy substitutions.

Then, in the following chapters, you'll find one hundred recipes designed to cut down on time, energy, and guesswork even further. Every recipe was created with those "I don't want to cook!" days in mind, so they require minimal active cooking time (meaning you might spend a short amount of time sautéing some vegetables, but the rest of the cooking is done in the oven, pressure cooker, or stove top—completely hands-off), little to no preplanning, and zero extra grocery store runs. Most importantly, these recipes are delicious, nutritious, and full of flavor.

DUCTION

Made from whole-food ingredients that you probably already have in your refrigerator, freezer, or pantry, these recipes include:

- Energizing breakfasts such as Slow Cooker Overnight Cinnamon Apple Steel-Cut Oats and 2-Minute "Fancy" Avocado Toast (Chapter 2)
- Satisfying lunches such as Buffalo Chicken Roll-Ups and Dill Pickle Tuna Melts on Rye Bread (Chapter 3)
- Simple sides such as Black Bean Sheet Pan Nachos and Parmesan-Crusted Broccoli Florets (Chapter 6)
- Pain-free dinners such as Shrimp and Andouille Sausage Boil with Corn and Red Potatoes and Korean-Inspired Beef and Rice Bowls with Cucumbers and Kimchi (Chapter 7)
- Mouthwatering desserts such as Campfire-Style Baked Banana Boats and Sweet and Salty Chocolate Bark (Chapter 8)
- And more!

Whether you're cooking for yourself or your family, or even if you're preparing a quick dish to share with friends, this book has everything you need for when you really don't want to cook but still want to eat—and eat well.

CHAPTER ONE

WHAT TO DO WHEN YOU JUST DON'T WANT TO COOK

15

Welcome to an easy way of optimizing the time you spend in your kitchen. Imagine preparing fresh, nutritious, and unbelievably delicious meals with very little prep time, minimal hands-on cooking time, and without using an abundance of dishes, pots, and pans. Combine the tools and tricks you will learn in this chapter with the recipes later in this book, and you are well on your way to a delicious *and fast* future in your kitchen.

Everyone has days when they just don't want to cook. Or maybe you never have the time or energy to think about (much less cook) a certain meal like breakfast or lunch. This chapter is here to help. In the pages that follow, you will learn how to cut down on prep work and cooking, properly store and reheat leftovers and make-ahead recipes, and ensure you always have pantry and fresh essentials on hand for quick and easy dishes.

The Top Three Secrets That Will Always Save You Time

Before getting into the different tricks, tools, and ingredients for easier prep work, cooking, and food shopping, there are a few key secrets every home cook should know. The three most important things to keep in mind when it comes to saving time and energy in the kitchen (without sacrificing taste!) are:

1 **Read through the recipe before starting.** This includes the instructions and any notes. This can save you so much time, especially if you are going to need to substitute ingredients (see more on substituting later in this chapter). This can't be stressed enough: Always start by reading through the full recipe.

2 **Mise en place.** *Mise en place* is a French phrase meaning "to put things in their place" and refers to the technique of measuring, cutting, prepping, and setting out the ingredients *before* beginning to make a recipe. While you might not want to take the time, doing the prep work before you start cooking will make the cooking process much quicker. It's also a surefire way to avoid missing an ingredient or step along the way (or worse, burning or overcooking something while you frantically try to grab that missing ingredient). Mise en place also includes gathering any utensils, mixing bowls, and pots and pans you will need. Once you get into the habit of setting everything out before cooking, you will see just how much time it saves you. You will learn more about the best prepping practices in the next section of this chapter.

3 **Consider whether you can double (or even triple) the recipe to freeze for a future meal.** It's a lot easier to cook once and eat two, three, four, five, or even six times by simply reheating something you already made than it is to cook a whole new meal. You will discover that a number of recipes in this book are perfect make-ahead and bulk meals.

Reading the recipe will always be your first step in the kitchen, mise en place the second. You can decide to double or triple the recipe during step one or once you see how much of each ingredient you have during step two. In the following sections, you will discover how to save even more time during step two, and how to ensure a quicker, less labor-intensive step three: cooking the recipe.

Save Time While Prepping Food

Setting out everything you will need before you start cooking already puts you ahead of having to rush to find ingredients and grab the right utensil before something burns. But there are other tools and easy tricks for cutting down on time *even* more as you prep.

Time-Saving Prep Tools

First up, tools. Most knife sets come with what are known as kitchen shears. Kitchen shears, or kitchen scissors, are food-safe scissors that easily click together and come apart into two separate pieces for thorough washing (or, better yet, tossing into the dishwasher). You can save effort in the kitchen by using kitchen shears to quickly cut items like fresh herbs, scallions, green beans (when they are too long), cooked chicken pieces, and more. Cut them right into the serving bowl or pan you are using to save time on cleanup. Just watch your fingers!

Have your baking sheet or dish ready to go when it comes time to cook by ensuring it is lined and/or greased if the recipe indicates. Baking sheets can be lined with either parchment paper or aluminum foil, and greased with nonstick cooking spray or the cooking oil you have on hand.

A digital scale is a game changer when it comes to quickly measuring items like chocolate chips, shredded cheese, and prepped vegetables. You can get a decent easy-to-read digital scale online for an affordable price.

You will find that almost every recipe in this book that uses garlic calls for it to be crushed. This saves you time, as crushing is a lot faster than slicing or chopping. For even less hassle, use a garlic press to crush one or two cloves at a time. No knife needed. A good garlic press is easy to find online at an affordable price. Look for a stainless steel garlic press that is very easy to clean and can go into the dishwasher to save even more effort.

Time-Saving Prep Tricks

When it comes to prepping ingredients, there are countless tricks for slicing, dicing, avoiding the knife and cutting board altogether, and more. You don't need to be a professional chef to chop onions like it's your job or find the best herbs at your local store. While the following tips aren't exhaustive, they are a great place to start.

Carrots

Some commonly used vegetables can be more labor-intensive to prepare than others. For example, peeling carrots can be very time-consuming and, let's be honest, annoying. A great way to avoid this is to buy organic carrots that look very fresh (check for graying, dark, or black marks or very dirty skin) and just giving the skins a good scrub before prepping for the recipe. Not only will you save time by avoiding peeling; you will get a nutrition boost because the carrot peels are packed with concentrated vitamin C and niacin.

Onions

Many of the recipes in this book use onions for flavor. One of the quickest ways to prepare raw onions for cooking is to halve and then thinly slice them. Just trim the ends, peel off the outer layer along with the skin, cut the onion in half from root to stem, place each half cut-side down, and use a sharp knife to slice. Chopped or diced onions can be more time-consuming. Some options to save significant time are to batch-chop the onions and freeze for future recipes. You can either batch-chop onions by hand or enlist the help of a food processor. Fit the food processor with the "S" or chopping blade, and prepare the onions by trimming the ends off, removing the outer layer with skin, and cutting into quarters. Load the onion quarters into the food processor in batches and press the Pulse button a few times until the onion pieces are roughly chopped. It is not recommended to press On or process fully, as the onions will quickly become watery. It's okay if the onion pieces are not perfectly uniform.

Divide the chopped onion into freezer-safe storage bags in the following portions:

- ½ cup chopped onion = 1 small onion
- 1 cup chopped onion = 1 medium onion
- 1½ cups chopped onion = 1 large onion
- 2 cups chopped onion = 1 extra-large onion

Chopped onions will stay fresh in the freezer for up to six months, as long as they are stored properly in freezer-safe bags or containers. When cooking with frozen chopped onions, do not defrost before using, just add an extra minute or two of cooking time for the onions to quickly defrost in the pan or pot, pour off any excess liquid that releases before moving on to the next step in the recipe. Another option is to buy packaged chopped or diced onion at the grocery store. This can be found with convenience vegetables like bagged spinach in the refrigerated section. Just note that since onions are very water-rich, packaged chopped onion doesn't have a long shelf life.

Shredded Cabbage and Bagged Prepped Vegetables

Shredded cabbage is another frequently used item in the recipes in this book. Most grocery stores sell bagged shredded cabbage, which is the ultimate time-saver. But, if you prefer to shred it yourself, try fitting a food processor with the shredding blade and loading long chunks of cabbage to shred faster than by hand. Store the shredded cabbage in a gallon storage bag (press out any extra air) in your refrigerator for up to five days. (Freezing shredded cabbage is not recommended, as it is so water-rich it loses its crunch and texture when it's defrosted.)

Packaged peeled, trimmed, cut, and prepped vegetables are *huge* time-savers, but you want to make sure you choose the freshest product available. Here are two simple tips:

1 Hold up bags or containers and look for excess moisture, discoloration, or graying on the ends of stems of items like broccoli florets, green beans, cauliflower, Brussels sprouts, and so on. These are indications that the vegetables are near the end of their life and should be avoided. You will want to pass on those and dig a bit for a better-looking package.

2 Check "packed on" or "sell by" dates to help you select the freshest vegetables available and get a sense of the remaining shelf life.

Rice

Not only is steamed rice an excellent side dish for many of the recipes in this book; it also takes only minutes to reheat in the microwave once cooked. Whether you prefer white rice or brown rice, they are totally interchangeable in these recipes. Just make sure to accommodate for a longer cook time if you make batches of brown rice to freeze. To save the most effort, check your grocery store freezer section for packaged cooked white or brown rice to store in your freezer. A more affordable option is to batch-cook rice once a week or once a month and freeze. After using your favorite cooking method, spread out the cooked rice on a baking sheet and pop it into the refrigerator. Once completely cooled, transfer the rice (in portions) to freezer-safe bags. To reheat, place frozen rice in a microwave-safe bowl with water (1 tablespoon per 4 cups of cooked rice) and cover with a moist paper towel. Microwave for 3–4 minutes, breaking up with a fork a few times during cooking, until heated through. Rice will keep in the freezer for up to six months.

Ginger

Dried ginger powder can be a good substitute for fresh gingerroot in recipes, but if you want to get the best ginger flavor, always opt for fresh gingerroot. The trick is, however, it doesn't actually have to be fresh—it can be frozen. This means you don't have to rush to use it days after purchase. Before freezing, wash the skin and pat dry with a paper towel. Tuck the cleaned ginger into a freezer-safe bag and remove any excess air from the bag. Whenever a recipe calls for ginger powder or fresh ginger, use a microplane to quickly grate the frozen ginger (skin included) in a dish, measure what you need, and refreeze the rest. You can substitute grated frozen gingerroot 50:1 for dried ginger powder, meaning for every ½ teaspoon of dried ginger powder, use 1 teaspoon of fresh or grated frozen gingerroot. Frozen gingerroot will keep in the freezer for up to six months.

Lemon and Lime Juice

Whenever a recipe calls for the juice of a lemon or lime, roll the uncut lemon or lime gently on a countertop or cutting board for 10–15 seconds to break down some of the cell walls. This will result in getting the maximum amount of juice from the fruit. If you plan to use a large amount of fresh lemon or lime juice for recipes, check your grocery store's juice aisle for a bottle of 100% lemon or lime juice. There should be no other ingredients. When squeezing fresh lemons or limes for juice that has to be measured, hold the cut lemon or lime over your cupped hand (over the dish you are using for the juice) to catch the seeds. It's much quicker to give your hand a rinse than it is to pick out every seed from a dish of juice!

Herbs

While many of the recipes in this book use dried herbs to save time, there are some cases where fresh herbs are recommended for the best result. Before chopping fresh herbs, sprinkle a tiny bit of kosher salt on top of the herbs on your cutting board to prevent them from flying all over the board and counter as you cut. Less mess, less time.

Butter

Keep butter at room temperature unless you live in a tropical climate. You will use less since it's easier to spread. For cooking, room-temperature butter melts much faster than cold butter and won't burn as quickly. If you prefer to keep your butter refrigerated, use this hack to quickly warm chilled butter: Place the amount you need on a small plate. Fill a drinking glass or mug with very hot water and then pour it back out. Turn the warmed, empty glass or mug over the butter and leave it there as a "dome" for a few minutes to warm the butter.

Other Staples

Some recipes use sticky pantry staples like peanut butter, maple syrup, or honey. Try spraying your measuring cup very lightly with nonstick cooking spray before measuring the sticky item to make cleanup quicker and easier.

Easy Substitutes

Despite all your prepping, you may not always have a certain ingredient for a recipe. Before heading out the door to make another trip to the grocery store, or giving up on the recipe altogether, consider whether you can substitute an ingredient you *do* have. Here are common ingredients you can replace with other easy-to-find options in a pinch:

- Sour cream: full-fat plain Greek yogurt (1:1).
- Mayonnaise: full-fat plain Greek yogurt, sour cream, or mashed avocado (1:1). Be aware that mayonnaise and avocado both have a unique flavor and texture, so the end result when using it will vary.
- Fresh herbs: dried herbs (2:1). As a general rule, use half the amount of dried herbs; this will vary depending on the herb and preferences.
- Ground beef or pork: ground turkey (1:1). Since ground turkey is a leaner meat, it's recommended to go with dark-meat ground turkey. Depending on the recipe, if you are substituting turkey for seasoned ground pork

like Italian sausage or andouille sausage, you may need to add an extra tablespoon of oil and some additional spices.

- Vegetable broth or beef broth: low-sodium chicken broth (1:1). When it comes to store-bought broth or stock, always buy the low-sodium option. It's much easier to add your own salt, as brands vary greatly in terms of salinity.

- Vegetable, beef, or chicken broth: 1 bouillon cube dissolved in 1 cup of boiling water or 1 tablespoon tamari mixed into 1 cup of water (any temperature).

Tamari: Japanese soy sauce, also called "shoyu" (1:1), or coconut aminos (1:1.33). Tamari is a salty, fermented, soybean-based sauce that is commonly used in Asian cooking. Shoyu is made with fermented soy and wheat, and tamari is made only with soybeans, so it is naturally gluten-free (always double-check the label if you have a gluten allergy). Coconut aminos are made from the sap of coconut blossoms and are frequently used as a substitute for soy sauce by people avoiding both gluten and soy. As coconut aminos tend to be a bit sweeter than shoyu or tamari, it's recommended to slightly increase the amount of coconut aminos used. So, for example, if a recipe calls for 2 tablespoons of tamari, use 3 tablespoons of coconut aminos.

Speed Thawing and Safe Defrosting

For those days when you don't have anything defrosted, try the cold water–bath technique to safely speed thaw meat, chicken, or fish. Remove all packaging from the frozen protein, place it in a plastic storage bag, and submerge sealed bag in a large bowl filled with cold water. The bag will probably float to the top, so place a heavy object on top to weigh it down. Check the protein every half an hour until it is thawed. Once thawed, remove from plastic bag and pat dry with a paper towel. Never use warm or hot water to do a quick thaw of frozen proteins, as the warm or hot water might encourage bacteria growth as well as change the texture of the meat by starting to "cook" the outside layer.

If you find that your uncooked poultry, meat, fish, or shrimp is vacuum-packed, it is highly recommended to remove the packaging *before* defrosting, especially for fish fillets. Vacuum sealing (also called ROP—Reduced Oxygen Packaging) is used to extend the shelf life of frozen foods by reducing odors and preventing some texture changes, which can sometimes result in spoilage. While this type of packaging helps keep your proteins fresher longer in the freezer, it is critical you remove it before defrosting because there is a risk of bacteria developing inside the packaging during thawing in the refrigerator. To defrost a package of vacuum-sealed meat or fish, simply cut it open, remove the frozen item, and place it in the refrigerator in a plastic storage bag or a container with a lid. Once defrosted, use paper towels to blot any excess moisture that has accumulated.

When defrosting meat of any kind, it's recommended to place the frozen package in a mixing bowl or on a rimmed plate to catch any juice that may drip as the package defrosts. This saves you time from having to disinfect your refrigerator in case of a leak.

Save Time While Cooking

Once you've read the recipe and done the prep work, it's time to get cooking. One of the most important steps before you put anything into a frying pan, wok, Dutch oven, or soup pot is to heat the pan or pot itself. Most pots and pans are made of stainless steel, cast iron, or ceramic coated–cast iron, and those surfaces need a minute or so to heat up and expand. Once expanded, the oil or butter fills the microscopic crevices on the surface, preventing sticking and assisting in better browning. Less sticking, less wasted food, and less cleanup time! This doesn't apply to nonstick pots and pans, however; these should only be used over medium or medium-low heat due to potential VOC (volatile organic compounds) being released.

Additionally, never overcrowd your pan if you are trying to crisp or brown food items. This goes for both meats and vegetables. Overcrowded pans tend to create a steam environment, resulting in soggy food. If you want a nice brown crust on those Boneless Taco-Seasoned Pork Chops with Pico de Gallo and Avocado (Chapter 7) or some crispy edges on those Skillet Green Beans with Balsamic Vinegar (Chapter 6), then make sure to give them plenty of space in the pan.

Whenever you need to bring a large pot of liquid to a boil, like for boiling pasta for Fusilli Pasta with Italian Sausage, Ricotta, and Baby Spinach or for Shrimp and Andouille Sausage Boil with Corn and Red Potatoes (both Chapter 7), put a lid on the pot. Placing a lid on a pot of water means the temperature of the water isn't impacted by the external air temperature, and it will boil much quicker.

When boiling water for wheat pasta, always generously salt the water before boiling to season the pasta from the inside out. A good rule of thumb is 2 tablespoons for 4 quarts of water and 1 pound of pasta. Never add oil to the water: It makes the pasta slippery so it won't "grab" the sauce. Also, never rinse wheat pasta after draining, as this rinses away the starch and prevents the sauce from sticking to the noodles. Keep in mind that other types of noodles such as rice noodles and udon noodles have their own instructions and may require omitting salt in the water and/or rinsing. Always read the package if the noodles are made from something other than wheat—it could save you a missed step or headache.

If you are cooking in the oven, always preheat the oven ahead of time to ensure even cooking time and avoid having to waste time waiting for the oven to come to temperature. Most household ovens can take anywhere from 10–15 minutes to reach full temperature. If you know you are going to be making Delicata Squash Pepperoni Pizza Boats (Chapter 7) for dinner, preheat the oven before you start mise en place.

When using baking sheets, line them with parchment paper (for temperatures up to 400°F) or tinfoil to save time cleaning up.

Always taste before adding more seasoning (such as salt, pepper, cumin, chili powder, and turmeric) to a recipe than is called for. There are many variables that can impact a recipe, like the salinity of broth, beans, canned tomatoes, different spice blends (like different brands of taco seasoning or "everything" seasoning). So, taste, taste, taste. Then adjust the seasoning if necessary. It is a lot easier to add more of a seasoning than to start something over because it is now too salty, spicy, or otherwise overwhelming.

Finally, even the best home cooks can sometimes misjudge a food's temperature when using only our eyes to guess. A good meat thermometer will not only save you time guessing when the food is at the correct temperature; it will also help avoid undercooked or overcooked food and frustration.

Shop Smart

The tips you've explored in this chapter can help cut down on grocery store runs; of course, you will still need to make a trip occasionally. Shopping smartly will make the process as painless as possible and ensure you have everything you need.

First things first: your shopping list. Whether you prefer a handwritten paper list or a digital list of some kind, if you frequent a specific grocery store regularly, you most likely know the layout of the store. Organizing your grocery list by aisles and store sections not only will save time while shopping (avoiding rushing back and forth for things); it will also be easier to stick to your list and avoid impulse purchases. Use the following tips to get the best quality for the items on your list.

Whenever a recipe calls for grated Parmesan, you want to use the good stuff to get the best possible flavor. Most American-made grated Parmesan isn't true Parmesan cheese and can sometimes have wood pulp or cellulose fiber added to it as a bulking agent. One way to avoid this is to look for the words "Parmigiano-Reggiano." Parmigiano-Reggiano is a legally protected designation of origin that's used only for Italian cheese. If you want a sheep's milk version of grated Parmesan, look for Pecorino Romano or Pecorino Locatelli, both of which are made from 100% sheep's milk. Pecorino Romano is usually aged under six months and is a bit tangier, whereas Pecorino Locatelli is aged longer and has a nuttier flavor. As a general rule, look for the real-deal Parmesan cheese in the deli area of the grocery store, not the sliced or brick cheese aisle.

For broth and canned tomato products, look for low-salt alternatives with labels that say "unsalted" or "low sodium." This way, *you* can control the salt and flavor with the spices used in the recipe.

One of the best convenience foods to have on hand is jarred pasta sauce. But, be warned: Jarred pasta sauce brands are not all the same. Read the labels and look for a sauce with minimal ingredients—preferably one that is free of sugar and stabilizers, and that has only ingredients you can pronounce and easily understand what they are for. Here is what such an ingredients label might look like: Italian Whole Peeled Tomatoes, Olive Oil, Onions, Salt, Garlic, Basil, Black Pepper, Oregano.

When it comes to nonstick cooking spray, look for a single-ingredient spray like olive oil or avocado oil. Read the label to avoid oil blends and highly refined seed oils, which can go rancid much quicker and ruin the taste of the recipe.

Get Cooking

Now that you've explored the essential secrets, ingredients, tools, and more for a faster, easier experience in the kitchen, it's time to get cooking! The recipes you will find in the following chapters share these features:

- Based on real food ingredients—no processed food, no artificial food, no junk food, and nothing with ingredients you can't pronounce or understand.

- Not overly complicated to make. In fact, every single recipe is streamlined and tested to eliminate any unnecessary steps and uses simple preparation techniques to save time.

- Use many of the same ingredients, like baby spinach, grape tomatoes, rotisserie chicken, and leftover or precooked frozen rice to make food shopping easier and allow you to whip up a variety of quick and delicious meals on the fly.

- Include prep times, active cook times (how much time is actively needed to prepare the recipe), and hands-off cook times (cooking that doesn't require active attention, such as waiting for a casserole to bake in an oven), so you know how many minutes to set aside for a recipe. You can use this information to pick the quickest recipes when you're in a crunch, as well as to choose longer recipes when you have a little more time to spare.

Refer to the information in this chapter as you make these dishes, and don't forget to read the Tips, Substitutions, Time-Savers, and More sections in the recipes that follow for even more guidance.

Now to dig into the truly delicious part of the book: the recipes!

CHAPTER TWO

READY, SET—BREAKFAST

Breakfast recipes do not need to be overcomplicated. You want fast, simple dishes that will fuel you for the morning and are loaded with flavor. In this chapter, you'll find quick and easy breakfasts that take less than 5 minutes to whip up, from a Fried Egg and Greens Breakfast Sandwich and NY Deli–Style Bagels and Lox, to a Greek Yogurt Parfait with Frozen Fruit and Honey Nuts and a No-Chop Spinach and Feta Omelet.

You'll also find several make-ahead breakfast recipes like Pepperoni Pizza Breakfast Casserole and Dill, Sweet Onion, and Everything Seasoning–Baked Omelet that you can prepare on the weekend and then enjoy for the whole week; reheat for 60–90 seconds, and it's ready to go. The make-ahead dishes also have minimal prep time so you won't be spending your weekend being overwhelmed in the kitchen. Start your day with a variety of whole-food breakfasts that will leave you feeling satisfied without a lot of effort.

Slow Cooker Overnight Cinnamon Apple Steel-Cut Oats

SERVES 6

Steel-cut oats are a nutritional powerhouse, but they take forever to make on the stove top. Spend just 5 minutes combining these ingredients into your slow cooker right before you go to bed, and you will wake up to a fantastic, warm breakfast ready to serve with your favorite toppings! You can substitute ¼ cup of brown sugar or coconut sugar for the maple syrup, or completely omit any sweetener from the cooking process and add your own when serving.

PREP TIME: 5 MINUTES ● ACTIVE COOK TIME: N/A ● HANDS-OFF COOK TIME: 8 HOURS

6 cups water

2 tablespoons ground cinnamon

1 teaspoon kosher salt

¼ cup pure maple syrup

1½ cups uncooked steel-cut oats

2 medium Gala apples, cored, seeded, and diced

4 tablespoons salted butter

1 Add water, cinnamon, salt, and maple syrup to a 3-quart or larger slow cooker. Whisk until well combined. Gently stir in oats and apple. Place butter on top of oat mixture.

2 Place lid on slow cooker and set to low for 8 hours. Stir well right before serving.

PER SERVING
Calories: 303 | Fat: 10g | Sodium: 450mg | Carbohydrates: 47g | Fiber: 7g | Sugar: 13g | Protein: 7g

Tips, Substitutions, Time-Savers, and More

For more texture, serve with something crunchy, like pecans, walnuts, or sliced almonds. Milk adds even more richness and flavor; just substitute half of the water for your milk of choice during cooking. And a drizzle of local honey or sprinkling of brown sugar on top adds a bit more sweetness. Don't have Gala apples? Any apple variety can be substituted.

NY Deli–Style Bagels and Lox

SERVES
4

There is nothing better than a NY deli–style bagel with lox! When it comes to smoked salmon, it's recommended that you use wild smoked salmon instead of Atlantic salmon. The lighter, orange-colored Atlantic salmon is more widely available and is cheaper but not necessarily better quality.

PREP TIME: 10 MINUTES ● ACTIVE COOK TIME: N/A ● HANDS-OFF COOK TIME: N/A

4 plain bagels, sliced and toasted

8 ounces cream cheese

8 ounces wild smoked salmon

1 medium English cucumber, sliced into rounds

1 medium red onion, peeled and thinly sliced

1/4 cup fresh dill leaves

8 turns (1/8 teaspoon) freshly ground black pepper

1 Allow toasted bagel halves to cool on a cutting board 2 minutes before spreading the cream cheese, so it doesn't melt.

2 Spread cream cheese evenly on bagel halves, then place equal amounts salmon on top.

3 Top each bagel half with cucumber, onion, and dill. Sprinkle with pepper. Serve.

PER SERVING
Calories: 605 | Fat: 23g | Sodium: 1,416mg | Carbohydrates: 64g | Fiber: 3g | Sugar: 4g | Protein: 28g

Tips, Substitutions, Time-Savers, and More

Where to buy good East Coast–style bagels depends on where you live. Start by looking up Jewish delis in your area. Avoid using whipped or light cream cheese, which have additives and gums that give it a chalky flavor. A thick schmear of regular cream cheese is best for a creamy, satisfying bagel. You can swap any savory type of bagel for plain bagels.

Pepperoni Pizza Breakfast Casserole

SERVES 8

Even though the prep time is short, this dish does need to bake for about an hour, which means that it is the perfect make-ahead breakfast. It freezes and reheats great. Pop this into the oven sometime on Sunday, and you'll have a full week's worth of breakfasts ready to be reheated!

PREP TIME: 7 MINUTES • ACTIVE COOK TIME: N/A • HANDS-OFF COOK TIME: 50 MINUTES

1 tablespoon extra-virgin olive oil

18 large eggs

1/2 teaspoon kosher salt

1/2 teaspoon Italian seasoning

1/4 teaspoon ground black pepper

1/4 teaspoon crushed red pepper flakes

3 ounces pepperoni rounds, roughly chopped

1 1/2 cups shredded mozzarella cheese, divided

1/2 cup pizza sauce

1 ounce small pepperoni rounds

Tips, Substitutions, Time-Savers, and More

If you can't find small pepperoni rounds, use kitchen scissors to cut large pepperoni rounds into small pieces. To reheat, microwave each slice 60–90 seconds at medium power before serving. To freeze: Place cut pieces on a baking sheet and set in the freezer. Once the pieces are individually frozen, transfer them to a freezer-safe bag or container.

1 Preheat oven to 350°F. Grease a 13" × 9" baking dish with oil.

2 In a large bowl, beat eggs until slightly foamy. Add salt, Italian seasoning, black pepper, and red pepper flakes. Add chopped pepperoni and 1 cup mozzarella. Mix to combine.

3 Pour egg mixture into prepared baking dish. Drizzle pizza sauce over casserole and top with remaining 1/2 cup mozzarella and whole pepperoni rounds.

4 Bake 45–50 minutes until center is firm to touch and edges are beginning to brown.

5 Remove from oven and allow to cool 10 minutes before slicing into eight pieces and serving.

PER SERVING
Calories: 303 | Fat: 19g | Sodium: 719mg | Carbohydrates: 4g | Fiber: 0g | Sugar: 1g | Protein: 22g

2-Minute "Fancy" Avocado Toast

SERVES
2

Avocado toast has been all the rage in recent years. And for good reason: It is truly one of the easiest and most delicious ways to use up a ripe avocado. You only need to add a few key pantry spices and a drizzle of olive oil to make a "fancy" version in 5 minutes.

PREP TIME: 5 MINUTES ● ACTIVE COOK TIME: N/A ● HANDS-OFF COOK TIME: N/A

2 (1/2"-thick) slices sourdough bread, toasted

1 medium avocado, peeled, pitted, and thinly sliced

2 teaspoons extra-virgin olive oil

1/4 teaspoon flake salt

1/8 teaspoon crushed red pepper flakes

8 turns (1/8 teaspoon) freshly ground black pepper

While toast is still hot, use a fork to mash avocado onto each slice of bread until evenly spread out. Drizzle with oil. Sprinkle with salt, red pepper flakes, and black pepper. Serve immediately.

PER SERVING
Calories: 228 | Fat: 15g | Sodium: 434mg | Carbohydrates: 20g | Fiber: 5g | Sugar: 2g | Protein: 4g

Tips, Substitutions, Time-Savers, and More

Test for avocado ripeness by popping off the stem at the top. A ripe avocado has a bright green color and is firm to the touch but not mushy. Save leftover avocado by placing it in a small bowl and completely submerging it in cold water. Cover and refrigerate until ready to use, up to 24 hours.

Fried Egg and Greens Breakfast Sandwich

SERVES 1

Save time by using a fried egg to make this hearty and nutritious greens-filled breakfast sandwich. No extra dish needed to beat an egg; just crack the egg directly into the pan. Serve topped with spinach and cheese between a toasted and buttered English muffin for a breakfast sandwich that tastes like it came from a deli!

PREP TIME: 2 MINUTES • ACTIVE COOK TIME: 5 MINUTES • HANDS-OFF COOK TIME: N/A

1 plain English muffin, split and toasted

1 tablespoon salted butter

1/2 tablespoon extra-virgin olive oil

1 ounce fresh baby spinach leaves

1 large egg

1/4 teaspoon kosher salt

8 turns (1/8 teaspoon) freshly ground black pepper

1 slice Cheddar cheese

Tips, Substitutions, Time-Savers, and More

No English muffins? You can substitute a toasted bagel or sliced bread, or layer the fried egg, spinach, and cheese into a tortilla. Use any cheese you have available as a substitute for Cheddar. Whole-leaf or chopped frozen spinach can be substituted for fresh. Allow an additional 2–3 minutes of cook time and make sure to drain off any excess liquid before adding the egg to the frying pan.

1 Butter toasted English muffin. Set aside.

2 Heat a medium nonstick or well-seasoned cast iron frying pan over medium heat 90 seconds. Once hot, add oil and spinach. Sauté spinach 90 seconds, stirring frequently, until fully wilted. Push cooked spinach to one side of pan.

3 Crack egg directly into other side of pan and sprinkle with salt and pepper. Cook 2 minutes.

4 Flip egg. Use tongs to pile spinach on top of egg, then top with cheese and half of buttered English muffin (buttered-side down). Gently press muffin down into cheese and continue cooking for 1 minute.

5 Use a spatula to transfer egg to remaining half of buttered muffin. Close sandwich and serve.

PER SERVING
Calories: 441 | Fat: 27g | Sodium: 1,189mg | Carbohydrates: 27g | Fiber: 3g | Sugar: 2g | Protein: 19g

Dill, Sweet Onion, and Everything Seasoning—Baked Omelet

SERVES 6

A baked omelet is a great hands-off way to feed a crowd or to line up breakfast for the next few days. This version combines eggs, fresh dill leaves, sliced sweet onion, and a finish of Everything Bagel seasoning. It's a delicious and protein-packed breakfast slice that can be reheated in 60 seconds.

PREP TIME: 5 MINUTES ● **ACTIVE COOK TIME: N/A** ● **HANDS-OFF COOK TIME: 55 MINUTES**

1 tablespoon salted butter

12 large eggs

$1/2$ teaspoon kosher salt

$1/2$ teaspoon ground black pepper

$1/2$ cup fresh dill leaves, roughly chopped

1 extra-large sweet onion, peeled, quartered, and thinly sliced into half-moons

1 tablespoon Everything Bagel seasoning

1. Preheat oven to 350°F. Grease an oven-safe 9" × 5$1/4$" loaf pan with butter.

2. In a large bowl, whisk eggs with salt and pepper until slightly foamy. Add in dill and onion. Mix until well combined.

3. Pour into prepared loaf pan. Sprinkle Everything Bagel seasoning evenly on top. Bake on center rack 50–55 minutes until center is firm.

4. Remove from oven and allow to cool in pan 15 minutes before slicing into six pieces and serving.

PER SERVING
Calories: 180 | Fat: 10g | Sodium: 512mg | Carbohydrates: 3g | Fiber: 0g | Sugar: 1g | Protein: 13g

Tips, Substitutions, Time-Savers, and More

Make this on the weekend and reheat a slice in the microwave on high for 60 seconds for a quick and filling breakfast on the go. It's excellent served with half an avocado or a few slices of tomato. Red onion can be substituted for the sweet onion. Two medium onions can be substituted for one extra-large onion.

Ham and Cheese 2-Minute Microwave Omelet

SERVES 1

This quick microwave omelet is the ultimate high-protein breakfast for super-busy mornings. Combine chopped or cubed deli ham and cheese with beaten eggs for a fully cooked 2-minute omelet that you can even take to go.

PREP TIME: 1 MINUTE ● ACTIVE COOK TIME: N/A ● HANDS-OFF COOK TIME: 2 MINUTES

2 large eggs

$1/8$ teaspoon kosher salt

8 turns ($1/8$ teaspoon) freshly ground black pepper

1 (1-ounce) slice ham, chopped

1 ($1/2$-ounce) slice Cheddar cheese, chopped

1 Combine eggs, salt, and pepper in a microwave-safe mug. Beat until slightly foamy, about 30 seconds. Mix in ham and cheese.

2 Microwave on high 2 minutes. Remove and allow to rest 2 minutes before serving.

PER SERVING
Calories: 246 | Fat: 15g | Sodium: 846mg | Carbohydrates: 2g | Fiber: 0g | Sugar: 0g | Protein: 21g

Tips, Substitutions, Time-Savers, and More

If you don't have Cheddar cheese, some good substitutions are Colby, pepper jack, American, Swiss, provolone, and feta. A slice of deli ham for sandwiches works great for this recipe, but leftover diced ham, ham steak, or Canadian bacon can also be used.

No-Chop Spinach and Feta Omelet

SERVES
2

A good omelet doesn't need to be overcomplicated! For this easy no-chop omelet, you save time by using bagged baby spinach leaves, a few spices, and crumbled feta cheese for a blast of flavor and added texture. Serve with sliced avocado or toast.

PREP TIME: 2 MINUTES ● ACTIVE COOK TIME: 4 MINUTES ● HANDS-OFF COOK TIME: 8 MINUTES

4 large eggs
1/2 teaspoon kosher salt
1/4 teaspoon ground black pepper
1/4 teaspoon dried oregano
1/4 teaspoon crushed red pepper flakes
2 tablespoons salted butter
3 ounces fresh baby spinach leaves
4 ounces Greek feta cheese, crumbled

1 Crack eggs into a small bowl. Add salt, black pepper, oregano, and red pepper flakes. Use a fork or small whisk to beat until slightly foamy (about 30 seconds).

2 Heat a 10" or 12" nonstick or well-seasoned cast iron pan over medium-low heat. Once hot, add butter.

3 Once butter is melted, 1–2 minutes, add spinach. Sauté 2 minutes, stirring constantly, until spinach is wilted. Use spatula to move spinach mixture to one side of the pan.

4 Pour egg mixture over spinach, tilting the pan so that egg spreads out evenly and covers spinach completely while the rest fills the pan.

5 Sprinkle feta over spinach half of eggs and let cook undisturbed for 6–8 minutes until eggs look mostly set.

Continued ▶

6 Use a spatula to gently fold plain half of eggs over spinach half and lightly press down with spatula 15 seconds.

7 Transfer to a serving plate, cut in half, and serve.

PER SERVING
Calories: 404 | Fat: 31g | Sodium: 1,367mg |
Carbohydrates: 5g | Fiber: 1g | Sugar: 3g | Protein: 22g

Tips, Substitutions, Time-Savers, and More

If you substitute frozen spinach (chopped or whole leaf) for the fresh spinach, add 3 minutes of cooking time. Frozen vegetables give off extra liquid, so note that the cooked omelet may have a slight green tint. That is okay—it is not recommended to pour off the extra spinach juice, as you will also wind up pouring off the butter.

Greek Yogurt Parfait with Frozen Fruit and Honey Nuts

SERVES 1

This easy Greek yogurt parfait is a delicious and quick breakfast. The genius is in the combination of flavors and textures. Thick, rich, full-fat Greek yogurt is layered with frozen wild blueberries. Wild blueberries are smaller than regular blueberries, so they defrost quicker and do not have to be chopped—that means they can be eaten directly from the freezer (time-saver!). Chopped nuts and honey complete this simple breakfast with the perfect amount of crunch and sweetness.

PREP TIME: 5 MINUTES ● ACTIVE COOK TIME: N/A ● HANDS-OFF COOK TIME: N/A

1/2 cup full-fat plain Greek yogurt

1 tablespoon frozen wild blueberries

1 tablespoon chopped pecans

2 teaspoons amber honey

Layer 1/4 cup Greek yogurt into the bottom of an 8-ounce drinking glass. Sprinkle with 1/2 tablespoon blueberries, followed by 1/2 tablespoon nuts, and 1 teaspoon honey. Repeat with remaining ingredients and serve immediately.

PER SERVING
Calories: 203 | Fat: 10g | Sodium: 40mg | Carbohydrates: 18g | Fiber: 1g | Sugar: 17g | Protein: 11g

Tips, Substitutions, Time-Savers, and More

Full-fat Greek yogurt is a must here for both flavor and texture. Make sure to buy plain, unsweetened yogurt. It's usually called "whole-milk" or "full-fat" depending on the brand. Pure maple syrup makes a great substitute for honey. Feel free to substitute chopped walnuts for the pecans.

4-Ingredient Banana Pancakes

SERVES 1

The secret to this easy pancake recipe is the 1:1 ratio of banana to egg. You can easily double, triple, or even quadruple this recipe to feed a crowd. Instead of panfrying in batches, use a large nonstick griddle to cook six or more pancakes at once.

PREP TIME: 1 MINUTE • ACTIVE COOK TIME: 7 MINUTES • HANDS-OFF COOK TIME: N/A

1 medium banana, peeled
1/4 teaspoon ground cinnamon
1/8 teaspoon kosher salt
1 large egg
1 tablespoon salted butter
1 tablespoon pure maple syrup

1 In a small bowl, mash banana. Add cinnamon, salt, and egg. Mix together until well combined but still chunky.

2 Heat a 12" nonstick or well-seasoned cast iron frying pan over medium heat. Once hot, add butter and melt, about 90 seconds.

3 Pour batter into two round shapes in pan. Cook undisturbed 3 minutes until bottom side is golden brown and the edges begin to look cooked. Gently flip and cook 2–3 more minutes until pancake is golden brown on both sides.

4 Transfer to a serving plate and serve hot drizzled with maple syrup.

PER SERVING
Calories: 330 | Fat: 15g | Sodium: 455mg | Carbohydrates: 41g | Fiber: 3g | Sugar: 27g | Protein: 8g

Tips, Substitutions, Time-Savers, and More
For an extra blast of flavor, add 1/2 teaspoon of pure vanilla extract to each batch of batter.

CHAPTER THREE
LESS-WORK LUNCHES

Lunchtime can often be overlooked or thought of as stressful when we are busy. It's time to stress less: Whether you are working from home and need a super-fast lunch or are packing lunch for school or work, this chapter is full of delicious lunch recipes that you can whip up with less work in no time!

You will find both warm and cold lunch recipes because being in a hurry or not feeling like cooking doesn't mean you have to eat the same thing every day. Use easy-to-find staples like tortillas and rotisserie chicken to create a nutrient-dense lunch in just minutes. Try a Rotisserie Chicken, Spinach, and Pickled Jalapeño Quesadilla that tastes better than takeout. Or capture the comforting flavor of deviled eggs in a Smashed Deviled Egg Sandwich that just requires some smashing and mixing—no worrying about having to carefully handle and fill eggs. Instead of skipping a meal to avoid the work, you'll look forward to making an easy and delicious dish that will keep you going through your day.

Dill Pickle Tuna Melts on Rye Bread

SERVES
2

This easy tuna melt is made in a frying pan in under 4 minutes! No need to turn on the oven or broiler. If you can't find unseeded Jewish deli rye bread, try sliced sourdough bread instead.

PREP TIME: 4 MINUTES • ACTIVE COOK TIME: 5 MINUTES • HANDS-OFF COOK TIME: N/A

1 (5-ounce) can unsalted dolphin-safe tuna, drained

2 tablespoons mayonnaise

2 tablespoons chopped dill pickles

1/2 teaspoon stone-ground mustard

1/4 teaspoon kosher salt

1/4 teaspoon ground black pepper

1/4 teaspoon dried dill

2 tablespoons salted butter, divided

4 slices unseeded Jewish rye bread

4 (1-ounce) slices sharp Cheddar cheese

1 In a medium bowl, combine tuna, mayonnaise, pickles, mustard, salt, pepper, and dill. Set aside.

2 Heat a 12" skillet over medium heat. Once hot, add 1 tablespoon butter. Once melted, about 90 seconds, add 2 slices bread. Add 1 slice cheese to each slice bread. Top each cheese slice with half of tuna mixture.

3 Spread remaining 1 tablespoon butter onto remaining 2 slices of bread. Place on tuna mixture, butter-side up. Cook 3 minutes.

4 Use a spatula to carefully flip each sandwich, then press down to flatten, and continue cooking 2 minutes until bread is browned.

5 Remove from heat, slice in half, and serve warm.

PER SERVING
Calories: 667 | Fat: 41g | Sodium: 1,503mg | Carbohydrates: 32g | Fiber: 4g | Sugar: 3g | Protein: 33g

Sriracha Tuna–Stuffed Avocado

SERVES 4

Transform canned tuna with just a handful of easy-to-find ingredients and a unique serving method. The spicy tuna can be made in advance and kept refrigerated in a covered container for up to 4 days.

PREP TIME: 10 MINUTES ● ACTIVE COOK TIME: N/A ● HANDS-OFF COOK TIME: N/A

2 (5-ounce) cans unsalted dolphin-safe tuna in water, drained

2 medium scallions, finely chopped

¼ cup mayonnaise

¼ cup sriracha

½ teaspoon lime juice

⅛ teaspoon kosher salt

2 medium avocados, pitted and halved

In a large mixing bowl, combine tuna, scallions, mayonnaise, sriracha, lime juice, and salt until well mixed. Divide evenly among avocado halves and serve immediately.

PER SERVING
Calories: 296 | Fat: 21g | Sodium: 607mg | Carbohydrates: 10g | Fiber: 5g | Sugar: 3g | Protein: 15g

Tips, Substitutions, Time-Savers, and More

Lemon juice can be substituted for lime juice. If you don't have either, apple cider vinegar will work. No avocados? Serve on large cucumber slices or crackers, or as a sandwich or wrap, atop a salad, or even stuffed into a halved bell pepper or plum tomato.

Smashed Deviled Egg Sandwiches

Everything you love and crave about deviled eggs without the extra work of carefully peeling, arranging, and stuffing the filling back into the egg halves. Just mash the hard-cooked eggs with some simple ingredients and serve on your favorite toasted bread with crunchy lettuce.

PREP TIME: 3 MINUTES ● ACTIVE COOK TIME: N/A ● HANDS-OFF COOK TIME: N/A

8 large eggs, hard-cooked and peeled

¼ cup mayonnaise

2 teaspoons yellow mustard

1 teaspoon Dijon mustard

1 teaspoon apple cider vinegar

¾ teaspoon kosher salt

½ teaspoon ground black pepper

½ teaspoon paprika

8 slices white sandwich bread, toasted

4 large romaine lettuce leaves

1 Use an egg slicer to slice eggs both horizontally and vertically into small pieces, or chop finely with a small knife. Transfer to a medium bowl and add mayonnaise, mustards, vinegar, and spices. Use a fork to smash and mix until well combined.

2 Divide among 4 toast slices. Top with lettuce and remaining 4 toast slices. Slice and serve immediately.

PER SERVING
Calories: 418 | Fat: 21g | Sodium: 1,002mg |
Carbohydrates: 32g | Fiber: 2g | Sugar: 5g |
Protein: 19g

Tips, Substitutions, Time-Savers, and More

For quick hard-boiled eggs, use the 5:3:5 pressure cooker method. Place eggs on an elevated rack in a pressure cooker along with 1 cup of water. Cover with lid and set to high pressure for 5 minutes. When the cooking time is up, set a timer for 3 minutes for natural pressure release. Make an ice bath by filling a large mixing bowl ¾ full with ice cubes and ice-cold water. Release remaining pressure and immediately transfer eggs with tongs to the ice bath for 5 minutes before peeling.

Curry Chickpea and Veggie Pita Pockets

SERVES
4

Smash chickpeas and combine with a bit of mayonnaise, chopped celery, spices, and red wine vinegar for an easy curry chickpea salad that is packed with flavor! Stuff into a pita pocket and finish with sliced tomato, red onion, and romaine lettuce leaves, and you have an easy lunch.

PREP TIME: 10 MINUTES ● ACTIVE COOK TIME: N/A ● HANDS-OFF COOK TIME: N/A

2 (15-ounce) cans chickpeas, rinsed and drained

2 medium celery stalks, chopped

$1/2$ cup mayonnaise

$1/2$ tablespoon red wine vinegar

1 teaspoon curry powder

$1/2$ teaspoon kosher salt

$1/4$ teaspoon ground black pepper

$1/4$ teaspoon ground turmeric

4 pita breads, sliced open

1 large vine-ripe tomato, cut into eight rounds

4 slices red onion

4 large romaine lettuce leaves

1 In a medium bowl, use a potato masher or fork to mash chickpeas until about $3/4$ are smashed.

2 Add celery, mayonnaise, vinegar, curry powder, salt, pepper, and turmeric. Mix until well combined.

3 Divide mixture into pita bread openings and top mixture with 2 slices tomato, 1 slice onion, and 1 lettuce leaf.

PER SERVING
Calories: 551 | Fat: 23g | Sodium: 1,076mg | Carbohydrates: 68g | Fiber: 11g | Sugar: 8g | Protein: 16g

Tips, Substitutions, Time-Savers, and More
Green leaf lettuce, red leaf lettuce, or iceberg lettuce all work in place of romaine. Or you can use a handful of baby spring mix. For some heat, add $1/4$ teaspoon cayenne pepper to the chickpea salad.

Pesto, Mozzarella, Spinach, and Roasted Pepper Baguette

SERVES 2

Grab a fresh baguette, and combine with prepared basil pesto, fresh mozzarella, baby spinach leaves, and jarred roasted peppers, and you are less than 5 minutes away from a tasty vegetarian sandwich worthy of any good sandwich shop menu.

PREP TIME: 5 MINUTES ● ACTIVE COOK TIME: N/A ● HANDS-OFF COOK TIME: 3 MINUTES

1 (12-ounce) baguette

$\frac{1}{2}$ cup basil pesto

1 (8-ounce) fresh mozzarella ball, sliced

$\frac{1}{2}$ ounce fresh baby spinach leaves

$\frac{1}{2}$ cup jarred roasted red peppers, drained and sliced into 1" strips

8 turns ($\frac{1}{8}$ teaspoon) freshly ground black pepper

1 Preheat oven to 400°F.

2 Place baguette in oven 3 minutes to slightly warm through and to make it easier to work with. Remove from oven and use a serrated knife to carefully slice baguette $^3/_4$ of the way through.

3 Spread pesto evenly on the insides of baguette. Layer mozzarella, spinach, red pepper pieces, and black pepper in bottom side of baguette.

4 Close top side of baguette and gently press down for 10 seconds. Cut into two or four sections and serve immediately.

PER SERVING
Calories: 1,014 | Fat: 42g | Sodium: 2,881mg | Carbohydrates: 104g | Fiber: 5g | Sugar: 10g | Protein: 49g

Tips, Substitutions, Time-Savers, and More

Store-bought basil pesto can really vary in flavor and quality. For the best flavor, look for a basil pesto that is refrigerated and fresh (not shelf-stable) and made with extra-virgin olive oil.

Hard-Cooked Egg Sammies with Everything Seasoning

SERVES
1

A simple sandwich that is packed with so much flavor and nutrition. This hard-cooked egg sandwich is a wonderful travel or hiking companion. Simply assemble, slice in half, wrap tightly in foil, and tuck away for up to 3 hours until ready to eat. Don't have sprouted Ezekiel bread? Substitute another robust, hearty bread like rye bread, seeded bread, or pumpernickel.

PREP TIME: 3 MINUTES ● ACTIVE COOK TIME: N/A ● HANDS-OFF COOK TIME: N/A

1 tablespoon salted butter

2 slices sprouted Ezekiel bread, lightly toasted

1 large hard-cooked egg, peeled and sliced

1/2 teaspoon Everything Bagel seasoning

Spread butter on toast slices. Layer egg on 1 bread slice, sprinkle with seasoning, and top with remaining slice buttered toast (butter-side down). Serve.

PER SERVING
Calories: 348 | Fat: 16g | Sodium: 463mg |
Carbohydrates: 31g | Fiber: 6g | Sugar: 1g | Protein: 16g

The Best BLT
(with Oven-Baked Bacon)

**SERVES
2**

A good BLT is all about the quality of the ingredients. And even with the best ingredients, it only takes 5 minutes to assemble! While crisp iceberg lettuce leaves are standard, you can substitute a bag of prewashed romaine lettuce leaves to save time.

PREP TIME: 4 MINUTES ● ACTIVE COOK TIME: N/A ● HANDS-OFF COOK TIME: 20 MINUTES

8 slices thick-cut bacon

4 tablespoons mayonnaise

4 slices white sandwich bread, lightly toasted

16 turns ($^1\!/_4$ teaspoon) freshly ground black pepper

1 large vine-ripe tomato, sliced

4 large leaves iceberg lettuce

Tips, Substitutions, Time-Savers, and More

If you happen to have leftover or precooked bacon, just reheat it in the microwave on high for 30 seconds. Look for ripe, vine-on, or in-season tomatoes for the best flavor possible.

1 Preheat oven to 400°F. On a lined baking sheet, arrange bacon slices in a single layer. Bake 20 minutes, turning once halfway through cook time. When done, carefully remove from oven and pat with a paper towel to remove excess grease.

2 Spread mayonnaise on each slice of toast. Sprinkle with pepper. Layer 4 slices bacon on 2 toast slices, breaking bacon in half if necessary.

3 Top with tomato and lettuce. Finish with remaining toast slices. Slice sandwiches diagonally and serve immediately.

PER SERVING
Calories: 690 | Fat: 45g | Sodium: 1,638mg | Carbohydrates: 36g | Fiber: 3g | Sugar: 7g | Protein: 30g

Rotisserie Chicken, Spinach, and Pickled Jalapeño Quesadilla

SERVES 2

Whip up this easy and flavor-packed quesadilla in under 10 minutes. The secret ingredient is the pickled jalapeños, which are widely available in most grocery stores and perfect to have on hand to add flavor to tacos, quesadillas, nachos, and more. Don't have shredded mozzarella cheese? Substitute shredded Cheddar, pepper jack, Mexican blend, or even Gruyère.

PREP TIME: 2 MINUTES ● ACTIVE COOK TIME: 7 MINUTES ● HANDS-OFF COOK TIME: N/A

2 (9") flour tortillas

4 ounces shredded mozzarella cheese, divided

10 pickled jalapeños

4 ounces rotisserie chicken, shredded

¼ cup fresh baby spinach leaves

1 Heat a 12" skillet over medium heat. Once hot, add 1 tortilla. Evenly layer with 2 ounces mozzarella. Top with jalapeños, chicken, and spinach. Top with remaining 2 ounces mozzarella and second tortilla.

2 Using a spatula, gently press down and continue cooking 3 minutes until cheese begins to melt.

3 Press down so melted cheese connects with the top tortilla (this makes it easier to flip) and then flip. Continue cooking 3–4 minutes until flipped side has browned and cheese is completely melted.

4 Remove from skillet, slice into eight pieces, and serve on two plates.

PER SERVING
Calories: 460 | Fat: 15g | Sodium: 1,251mg | Carbohydrates: 42g | Fiber: 2g | Sugar: 4g | Protein: 35g

Hummus, Veggie, and Feta Wrap

SERVES
1

Use your favorite tortilla (you can substitute gluten-free or even grain-free tortillas) to create a vibrant and tasty vegetarian lunch wrap in 5 minutes. Goat cheese can be substituted for feta cheese. Prefer no cheese? Omit the cheese and substitute sliced avocado for a vegan version. For a kick of heat, a dash or two of hot sauce on top of the hummus is excellent! Feel free to use your favorite flavor of hummus.

PREP TIME: 5 MINUTES • ACTIVE COOK TIME: N/A • HANDS-OFF COOK TIME: N/A

1 (9") flour tortilla

2 tablespoons plain hummus

1 ounce Greek feta cheese, crumbled

6 mint leaves

1 ounce shredded carrots

1 ounce thinly sliced English cucumber

¼ cup spring mix

1 Heat a 12" skillet over medium heat until hot. Add tortilla and cook 15–20 seconds on each side until warmed up and easier to fold.

2 Remove tortilla to a cutting board or dinner plate. Spread hummus evenly over warmed tortilla. Sprinkle with feta, mint, carrots, and cucumber. Top with spring mix.

3 Fold bottom of tortilla up about 1" to create a pocket. Roll tortilla from one side, pushing all the vegetables down and tightening the roll as you meet the other side. Serve.

PER SERVING
Calories: 349 | Fat: 13g | Sodium: 906mg |
Carbohydrates: 46g | Fiber: 5g | Sugar: 5g | Protein: 13g

Buffalo Chicken Roll-Ups

Craving the flavor of buffalo chicken but short on time? These Buffalo Chicken Roll-Ups are the perfect solution. You only need some easy-to-find ingredients, and you are 10 minutes away from a simple and nourishing meal that will satisfy that buffalo chicken craving. You can substitute gluten-free or grain-free wraps of choice for the tortillas.

PREP TIME: 10 MINUTES • ACTIVE COOK TIME: N/A • HANDS-OFF COOK TIME: N/A

12 ounces cubed rotisserie chicken

½ cup mayonnaise

2 medium celery stalks, chopped

2 tablespoons Frank's RedHot Original Cayenne Pepper Sauce

4 (9") flour tortillas

4 large leaves romaine lettuce

1 Combine chicken, mayonnaise, celery, and hot sauce in a large bowl. Set aside.

2 Heat a 12" skillet over medium heat. Once hot, add 1 tortilla. Warm 20 seconds on each side. This makes the tortillas easier to fold and handle without breaking and cracking. Repeat until all tortillas are warm.

3 Remove each tortilla to a serving plate. Top with chicken salad and lettuce. Fold up the bottom of each tortilla and roll lengthwise. Serve immediately.

PER SERVING
Calories: 522 | Fat: 26g | Sodium: 1,198mg |
Carbohydrates: 39g | Fiber: 3g | Sugar: 3g |
Protein: 30g

CHAPTER FOUR

SUPER-EASY SALADS

There has long been a myth that great salads need to have lots of ingredients and be complicated to make. This chapter is here to prove that is not true. Just look at the Everyday Simple Dinner Salad: This is a no-chop, no-work basic salad that you can serve with literally *any* meal. (In fact, you will find this easy, everyday salad recipe repeated throughout Chapter 7: Dinners That Don't Take All Day.) Use this recipe whenever you need to add a vegetable to a meal and don't have time to cook a hot side dish. And if you have kids, this is the perfect way to get them involved: It's so easy, even little kids can make it by themselves.

In the mood for something that looks like it takes a lot of effort (but doesn't)? You will find a recipe for 5-Minute Authentic Greek Salad that tastes like it came from a restaurant. You'll learn how to use rotisserie chicken to make an absolutely delicious herbed chicken salad in no time, as well as how to create a No-Chop Mediterranean Pasta Salad that is ready just a few minutes after the pasta is cooked. Both the Shrimp and Avocado Salad with Sweet Corn and the Arugula, Avocado, Strawberry, and Pecan Salad with Balsamic also look worthy of a fancy restaurant but are ready in less than 10 minutes.

Everyday Simple Dinner Salad

If you often feel like you don't have the time (or energy) to make a salad or get a vegetable on the table as a side to dinner, this Everyday Simple Dinner Salad is just the ticket. And you can always add to the base salad when you have more time by adding chopped cucumber, grape tomatoes, sliced onion, or sliced peppers into the mix.

PREP TIME: 3 MINUTES • ACTIVE COOK TIME: N/A • HANDS-OFF COOK TIME: N/A

4 loosely packed cups spring mix or 50/50 salad mix

$1/4$ cup shredded carrots

$1/4$ cup shredded green cabbage

$1/4$ teaspoon kosher salt

8 turns ($1/8$ teaspoon) freshly ground black pepper

$1/4$ cup extra-virgin olive oil

2 tablespoons balsamic vinegar

Combine all ingredients in a large bowl. Serve immediately.

PER SERVING
Calories: 135 | Fat: 13g | Sodium: 175mg | Carbohydrates: 3g | Fiber: 1g | Sugar: 2g | Protein: 1g

Tips, Substitutions, Time-Savers, and More

Make those containers of salad mix last longer by layering two or three paper towels in the container to absorb excess moisture. Always check the "use by" or "packed on" date on the packages of prewashed lettuce and make sure to turn over the container and look for wet or black lettuce to avoid buying a rotten package.

No-Chop Mediterranean Pasta Salad

SERVES 6

One of the tricks to making a delicious pasta salad is seasoning the pasta while it's still warm. This Mediterranean pasta salad is filled with a variety of colors, textures, and flavors—and you don't have to chop a single thing! It is excellent served warm or chilled. Swap out the penne for any short pasta you prefer, such as fusilli, orecchiette, or elbow.

PREP TIME: 8 MINUTES ● ACTIVE COOK TIME: N/A
● HANDS-OFF COOK TIME: 10 MINUTES (ACCORDING TO PASTA DIRECTIONS)

$\frac{1}{2}$ cup extra-virgin olive oil

$\frac{1}{4}$ cup balsamic vinegar

$1\frac{1}{2}$ teaspoons kosher salt

1 teaspoon ground black pepper

$\frac{1}{2}$ teaspoon crushed red pepper flakes

1 (15-ounce) can cannellini beans, rinsed and drained

2 (5-ounce) cans unsalted dolphin-safe tuna in water, drained

$\frac{1}{3}$ cup sliced and drained kalamata olives

1 cup drained roasted red peppers, chopped or pulled apart into bite-sized pieces

4 ounces fresh baby spinach leaves

1 pound uncooked penne pasta

1 Set a large pot of salted water to boil over high heat.

2 While water is coming to a boil, add oil, vinegar, salt, black pepper, and red pepper flakes to a large bowl. Use a fork or whisk to mix well.

3 Add beans, tuna, olives, and red pepper pieces to bowl, stir to combine, and set aside.

4 Place a large strainer in the sink and add spinach to strainer. Set aside.

5 Once water is boiling, cook pasta according to package directions.

6 Strain pasta over spinach. Immediately transfer to bowl with bean and tuna mixture.

7 Use a wooden spoon or spatula to toss until everything is well coated in oil and spices.

Continued ▶

8   Cover bowl with plastic wrap and refrigerate until ready to serve, up to 4 days.

9   Before serving, mix thoroughly to redistribute any oils that settled at the bottom of the bowl.

PER SERVING
Calories: 581 | Fat: 21g | Sodium: 1,392mg | Carbohydrates: 72g | Fiber: 8g | Sugar: 4g | Protein: 24g

Tips, Substitutions, Time-Savers, and More

When bringing a pot of water to a boil, cover it with a lid so the water will boil quicker. If you can't find sliced kalamata olives, substitute with sliced black olives. Make this gluten-free by substituting your favorite gluten-free pasta. Jovial brand is recommended for the best consistency and texture. Add 4 ounces crumbled feta cheese for even more flavor, color, and texture.

Rotisserie Chicken Salad with Fresh Herbs

SERVES 4

Add a rotisserie chicken to your cart every shopping trip: this cooked, tender meat is so versatile. Use cubed rotisserie chicken and simple herbs to create a tasty meal in 10 minutes. This recipe is excellent served with crackers; as a sandwich; alongside a salad; as lettuce wraps; or stuffed into a halved tomato, bell pepper, or avocado.

PREP TIME: 10 MINUTES • ACTIVE COOK TIME: N/A • HANDS-OFF COOK TIME: N/A

12 ounces cubed rotisserie chicken

$1/2$ cup mayonnaise

2 tablespoons finely chopped flat-leaf parsley

$1/2$ teaspoon kosher salt

$1/2$ teaspoon dried dill

$1/4$ teaspoon ground black pepper

2 medium celery stalks, chopped

In a large bowl, combine all ingredients. Serve immediately or chilled.

PER SERVING
Calories: 307 | Fat: 22g | Sodium: 748mg | Carbohydrates: 1g | Fiber: 0g | Sugar: 0g | Protein: 24g

Tips, Substitutions, Time-Savers, and More

This recipe can be refrigerated in a covered container for up to 4 days. Fresh cilantro can be substituted for parsley. Fresh dill can be substituted for dried dill; use 2 tablespoons finely chopped fresh dill in place of the $1/2$ teaspoon dried dill. Look for a high-quality jarred mayonnaise that is made from avocado oil or extra-virgin olive oil.

Chilled Peanut Noodle Salad with Cucumbers and Chicken

SERVES
4

This easy peanut noodle salad comes together in just about 15 minutes. It's the perfect make-ahead meal since it is best served chilled. You can whip this up in the morning before work or even the night before and have dinner ready as soon as you get home with no extra work.

PREP TIME: 10 MINUTES ● ACTIVE COOK TIME: N/A ●
HANDS-OFF COOK TIME: 5 MINUTES (ACCORDING TO NOODLE DIRECTIONS)

For Peanut Sauce

½ cup creamy unsweetened peanut butter

2 tablespoons toasted sesame oil

2 tablespoons rice vinegar

2 tablespoons pure maple syrup

2 tablespoons warm water

1 tablespoon tamari

½ tablespoon sriracha

2 cloves garlic, peeled and crushed

½ teaspoon kosher salt

¼ teaspoon ground black pepper

1 *To make Peanut Sauce:* In a small bowl, combine all ingredients. Set aside.

For Noodles

1 (12-ounce) package uncooked udon noodles

8 ounces shredded rotisserie chicken

1 medium English cucumber, sliced into half-moons

2 medium scallions, thinly sliced

¼ cup roughly chopped roasted salted peanuts

2 *To make Noodles:* Cook noodles according to package directions.

3 Transfer noodles to a large bowl, add Peanut Sauce, and use tongs to gently lift and mix noodles until well coated.

4 Add chicken, cucumber, scallions, and peanuts and toss to combine. Cover bowl with plastic wrap and refrigerate at least 1 hour (up to overnight).

5 Once chilled, let rest on the counter 20 minutes before serving. Use tongs to toss just before serving to redistribute any settled Peanut Sauce.

PER SERVING
Calories: 725 | Fat: 28g | Sodium: 1,044mg | Carbohydrates: 82g | Fiber: 5g | Sugar: 16g | Protein: 37g

Tips, Substitutions, Time-Savers, and More

You can substitute spaghetti or linguine for the udon. For a gluten-free version, substitute 100% buckwheat soba noodles or thick rice noodles. Cooked shrimp or thinly sliced beef or pork can be substituted for rotisserie chicken. Or, for a totally vegan version, omit the chicken and add cubed, baked tofu. Avoiding peanuts? Try roasted almond butter and chopped salted, roasted almonds.

Arugula, Avocado, Strawberry, and Pecan Salad with Balsamic

SERVES 4

An easy salad that looks fancy! Combine a bag of prewashed arugula with fresh avocado, sliced red onion, strawberries, and pecans (which can be left whole or chopped). Top with a simple vinaigrette of olive oil and balsamic vinegar, and you have a stunning dish in 10 minutes.

PREP TIME: 10 MINUTES ● ACTIVE COOK TIME: N/A ● HANDS-OFF COOK TIME: N/A

2 tablespoons sliced red onion

1/4 cup extra-virgin olive oil

2 tablespoons balsamic vinegar

1/2 teaspoon kosher salt

1/4 teaspoon ground black pepper

4 ounces bagged arugula

1 large avocado, peeled, pitted, and thinly sliced

12 medium strawberries, hulled and sliced from top to bottom

1/4 cup pecans

1 Place onions in a small bowl of cold water and let sit 5 minutes.

2 In a small jar, add oil, vinegar, salt, and pepper. Whisk or cover and shake until well combined. Set aside.

3 On a large serving platter, layer arugula, avocado, strawberries, drained onions, and pecans. Serve with vinaigrette on the side for drizzling.

PER SERVING
Calories: 250 | Fat: 23g | Sodium: 302mg | Carbohydrates: 10g | Fiber: 4g | Sugar: 4g | Protein: 2g

Tips, Substitutions, Time-Savers, and More

Plate this salad on a flat platter for the best presentation and easy serving. This ensures everyone gets a section with all of the toppings and that they don't fall to the bottom of a bowl. Roasted or candied pecans are a great substitute for plain pecans.

Caprese Pasta Salad

Combine the flavor of caprese salad with orecchiette pasta for a Caprese Pasta Salad that is a meal in a bowl. Grape or cherry tomatoes save time and are the perfect size for each forkful. Mini fresh mozzarella balls are ideal in terms of size, but you can easily substitute cubed fresh mozzarella if you can't find them. A delicious and easy dish in 20 minutes.

**PREP TIME: 8 MINUTES ● ACTIVE COOK TIME: N/A ●
HANDS-OFF COOK TIME: 12 MINUTES (ACCORDING TO PASTA DIRECTIONS)**

12 ounces uncooked orecchiette pasta

½ cup extra-virgin olive oil

¼ cup balsamic vinegar

2 teaspoons kosher salt

½ teaspoon ground black pepper

1 pound grape tomatoes, halved from top to bottom

8 ounces fresh mini mozzarella balls, halved

1 ounce (about 1 cup packed) thinly sliced fresh basil leaves

1 Bring a large pot of salted water to a boil over high heat. Once boiling, cook pasta according to package directions.

2 While pasta cooks, whisk oil, vinegar, salt, and pepper in a large bowl until well combined. Add tomatoes, mozzarella, and basil leaves. Stir and set aside.

3 Once pasta is cooked, immediately drain and add to bowl. Toss until well coated. Serve.

PER SERVING
Calories: 570 | Fat: 26g | Sodium: 1,140mg | Carbohydrates: 63g | Fiber: 4g | Sugar: 5g | Protein: 18g

Tips, Substitutions, Time-Savers, and More

This recipe can be served warm or cold. If serving chilled, store in a covered container in the refrigerator. Remove from refrigerator and let rest on the counter 20 minutes before serving. Toss pasta from the bottom right before serving to redistribute any settled oil and vinegar mixture.

White Bean Salad with Goat Cheese and Arugula

SERVES
4

Canned white beans are the base of this flavor-packed vegetarian salad. A simple dressing of good olive oil, lemon juice and zest, crushed garlic, and a few spices is tossed with the white beans and baby arugula and topped with crumbled goat cheese. This salad is excellent served with a crusty baguette or a thick slice of sourdough bread.

PREP TIME: 6 MINUTES ● ACTIVE COOK TIME: N/A ● HANDS-OFF COOK TIME: N/A

¼ cup extra-virgin olive oil

Zest and juice of 1 large lemon

1 clove garlic, peeled and crushed

1 teaspoon kosher salt

½ teaspoon ground black pepper

½ teaspoon Dijon mustard

¼ teaspoon crushed red pepper flakes

2 (15-ounce) cans cannellini beans, rinsed and drained

1 ounce baby arugula

4 ounces goat cheese, crumbled

1 In a medium bowl, combine oil, lemon zest and juice, garlic, salt, black pepper, mustard, and red pepper flakes. Add beans and arugula. Toss until coated.

2 Divide onto four serving plates or bowls and top each serving with goat cheese.

PER SERVING
Calories: 368 | Fat: 22g | Sodium: 1,118mg | Carbohydrates: 33g | Fiber: 13g | Sugar: 0g | Protein: 17g

5-Minute Authentic Greek Salad

SERVES 4

Since authentic Greek salad isn't traditionally served on lettuce, you won't have to spend any time cleaning or preparing it for this dish. Combine ripe plum tomatoes with red onion, cucumber, green pepper, olives, and feta cheese. Top with dried oregano, olive oil, and a bit of red wine vinegar, and you have a delicious, easy, and quick salad that everyone will love.

PREP TIME: 10 MINUTES • ACTIVE COOK TIME: N/A • HANDS-OFF COOK TIME: N/A

1 pound ripe plum tomatoes, cut into quarters

1 small red onion, peeled and cut into rings

2 medium English cucumbers, cut into thick half-moons

1 large green bell pepper, halved, seeds and ribs removed, cut into $1/2$" strips

24 pitted kalamata olives

8 ounces Greek feta cheese, crumbled

$1 1/2$ teaspoons dried oregano

$1/4$ cup extra-virgin olive oil

1 tablespoon red wine vinegar

1 On a large serving platter, layer tomatoes, onion, cucumber, pepper, and olives.

2 Sprinkle feta and oregano over the vegetables.

3 In a small measuring cup, combine oil and vinegar. Pour over salad right before serving.

PER SERVING
Calories: 395 | Fat: 33g | Sodium: 990mg | Carbohydrates: 15g | Fiber: 3g | Sugar: 9g | Protein: 11g

Tips, Substitutions, Time-Savers, and More

Serve with fresh pita bread or a sliced crusty baguette. You can substitute 1 pound of halved cherry or grape tomatoes for the plum tomatoes. One medium English cucumber can be swapped for standard garden cucumbers. It's not recommended to buy crumbled feta as powdered cellulose or another form of an anticaking agent is usually added. These additives can make the crumbled feta dry and change the texture and taste.

The Easiest Taco Salad

SERVES 4

Crisp romaine lettuce is topped with black beans, pico de gallo, shredded cheese, diced avocado, crunchy tortilla chips, and taco meat to make this quick, tasty salad. Save time by purchasing premade pico de gallo and substituting prepared guacamole for the sliced avocado. For a creamy version, drizzle 1 or 2 tablespoons of sour cream or Greek yogurt over the dish right before serving.

PREP TIME: 5 MINUTES ● ACTIVE COOK TIME: 16 MINUTES ● HANDS-OFF COOK TIME: N/A

1 pound 80% lean ground beef

2 tablespoons mild taco seasoning

1/2 cup water

2 (10-ounce) bags chopped or shredded romaine lettuce

1 (15-ounce) can black beans, rinsed and drained

1 cup pico de gallo

1 cup shredded Mexican-style cheese

1 large avocado, peeled, pitted, and diced

4 ounces tortilla chips

1. Heat a 12" skillet over medium-high heat. Once hot, add ground beef. Cook 5–6 minutes, stirring frequently and breaking up beef with a wooden spoon or spatula, until most of the pink is gone.

2. Strain any excess fat from pan and add taco seasoning and water to pan. Stir to combine and raise heat to high.

3. Once water is bubbling, lower heat to medium and cook 8–10 minutes, stirring occasionally, until the water is mostly evaporated.

4. While meat is cooking, divide remaining ingredients among four serving bowls and set aside.

5. Once meat is done, remove pan from heat and allow to cool 5 minutes before adding equal amounts to bowls. Serve immediately.

Tips, Substitutions, Time-Savers, and More

Swap ground turkey or ground chicken for ground beef. The taco meat can be made up to 48 hours ahead of serving and warmed in the microwave right before plating. For a vegetarian version, try omitting the ground meat and doubling the beans to 2 cans. To add that signature taco flavor, look for seasoned black beans instead of plain black beans.

PER SERVING
Calories: 752 | Fat: 30g | Sodium: 1,348mg | Carbohydrates: 70g | Fiber: 22g | Sugar: 7g | Protein: 44g

Deconstructed Hummus Salad with Cucumber and Tomato

SERVES 4

Create a delicious and satisfying salad that is loaded with nutritious vegetables and has all the flavors of hummus.

¼ cup extra-virgin olive oil

2 tablespoons freshly squeezed lemon juice

2 tablespoons tahini

1 teaspoon dried parsley

1 teaspoon ground cumin

¾ teaspoon kosher salt

¼ teaspoon ground black pepper

¼ teaspoon paprika

2 cloves garlic, peeled and crushed

2 (15-ounce) cans garbanzo beans, rinsed and drained

1 pound grape tomatoes, halved

1 medium English cucumber, quartered and sliced into ½" pieces

1 In a medium bowl, add oil, lemon juice, tahini, spices, and garlic. Whisk until well combined.

2 Add beans, tomatoes, and cucumber to oil and spice mixture. Toss to coat. Serve immediately or store in a covered container in the refrigerator until ready to use, up to 48 hours.

PER SERVING
Calories: 375 | Fat: 19g | Sodium: 719mg | Carbohydrates: 40g | Fiber: 11g | Sugar: 10g | Protein: 12g

Tips, Substitutions, Time-Savers, and More

This salad is excellent served with fresh or toasted pita bread on the side. One tablespoon of fresh chopped parsley can be substituted for dried parsley for an extra pop of flavor.

Shrimp and Avocado Salad with Sweet Corn

SERVES 3

Save time and prep work by using frozen, uncooked, peeled, and deveined shrimp and frozen sweet corn kernels. Boil them together and toss with fresh avocado, red onion, basil, and a simple lemon olive oil dressing for a showstopper salad that is practically effortless.

PREP TIME: 7 MINUTES ● ACTIVE COOK TIME: N/A ● HANDS-OFF COOK TIME: 4 MINUTES

⅓ cup extra-virgin olive oil

2 tablespoons freshly squeezed lemon juice

1 teaspoon kosher salt

½ teaspoon ground black pepper

1 pound frozen, uncooked, peeled, deveined large shrimp

1 cup frozen yellow sweet corn kernels

½ medium red onion, peeled, halved, and thinly sliced

1 ounce (about 1 cup packed) thinly sliced fresh basil leaves

1 large avocado, peeled, pitted, and diced

1. In a large mixing bowl, combine oil, lemon juice, salt, and pepper. Set aside.

2. Bring a medium pot of salted water to a boil over high heat. Once boiling, add shrimp and corn. Continue boiling 3–4 minutes until shrimp are cooked through and pink.

3. Immediately drain shrimp and corn and add to bowl with oil mixture. Toss to coat.

4. Add onion, basil, and avocado to shrimp mixture. Gently toss to combine and serve immediately.

PER SERVING
Calories: 446 | Fat: 31g | Sodium: 1,830mg | Carbohydrates: 18g | Fiber: 5g | Sugar: 2g | Protein: 23g

Rotisserie Chicken Mason Jar Salads

SERVES 4

Put Mason jars to use by building ready-to-eat salads for easy lunches or dinners throughout the week. The key to making Rotisserie Chicken Mason Jar Salads is to layer the ingredients by density. Keep the jars upright until you are ready to serve, then simply shake the contents, pour into a serving bowl, and eat!

PREP TIME: 10 MINUTES • ACTIVE COOK TIME: N/A • HANDS-OFF COOK TIME: N/A

8 tablespoons extra-virgin olive oil

4 tablespoons balsamic vinegar

$1/2$ teaspoon kosher salt

16 turns ($1/4$ teaspoon) freshly ground black pepper

12 ounces cubed rotisserie chicken

$1/2$ cup shredded green cabbage

$1/2$ cup shredded carrots

4 cups bagged mixed greens

4 tablespoons sliced almonds

1 Divide oil, vinegar, salt, and pepper into four quart-sized Mason jars. Next, layer equal amounts chicken, cabbage, carrots, and mixed greens in each jar. Top with 1 tablespoon almonds per jar.

2 Cover and refrigerate jars until ready to use, up to 5 days. Prior to serving, shake the jar until the contents are fully coated by the dressing, then pour into a serving bowl or eat directly out of the jar.

PER SERVING
Calories: 415 | Fat: 31g | Sodium: 594mg | Carbohydrates: 7g | Fiber: 2g | Sugar: 4g | Protein: 26g

CHAPTER FIVE

SERIOUSLY SIMPLE SOUPS

Homemade soup doesn't have to be intimidating. In fact, with a few handy shortcuts, a delicious, comforting whole-foods pot of warming soup can happen in your kitchen in no time. By the end of this chapter, you will be whipping up seriously simple recipes with minimal effort!

It is common for soup recipes to start with a base of chopped onion, carrot, and celery. This combination is called mirepoix, and it can be the most time-consuming step when beginning a homemade soup recipe. But since many grocery stores now sell mirepoix in the convenience vegetables section, you can save a lot of time by adding a package to your grocery cart. Some food stores also sell a frozen version of mirepoix, which is excellent to keep stashed in the freezer for a last-minute pot of soup. You can also use a food processor to create your own mirepoix in minutes. You'll use these cooking shortcuts and more to make the flavor-packed recipes in this chapter, from Lasagna Soup with Italian Sausage, Fresh Basil, and Grated Parmesan and Chicken Noodle Soup with Fresh Thyme, to Pressure Cooker Beef Barley Stew, all in around 30 minutes.

Red Lentil Soup with Shredded Cabbage

SERVES 6

Quick-cooking red lentils break down almost completely in 20 minutes, delivering a creamy and indulgent-tasting vegetarian soup with nutritious ingredients. This recipe is excellent served with a drizzle of extra-virgin olive oil on top and some crusty bread.

PREP TIME: 5 MINUTES ● ACTIVE COOK TIME: 5 MINUTES ● HANDS-OFF COOK TIME: 20 MINUTES

1/4 cup extra-virgin olive oil

1 large yellow onion, peeled and chopped

6 cloves garlic, peeled and crushed

2 medium celery stalks, cut into 1/8" half-moons

1 tablespoon kosher salt

1 teaspoon ground cumin

3/4 teaspoon ground black pepper

3/4 teaspoon chili powder

1/2 teaspoon ground turmeric

2 cups uncooked red lentils, rinsed

8 cups low-sodium vegetable broth

1 (14.5-ounce) can unsalted diced tomatoes, including juice

1 (10-ounce) bag shredded green cabbage

1 Heat a large soup pot over medium heat. Once hot, add oil, onion, garlic, celery, and spices. Sauté 5 minutes, stirring occasionally.

2 Add lentils, broth, and tomatoes to pot. Raise heat to high and bring to a boil.

3 Once boiling, add cabbage, cover, and reduce heat to a simmer. Simmer 20 minutes. Serve hot.

PER SERVING
Calories: 381 | Fat: 10g | Sodium: 1,398mg | Carbohydrates: 56g | Fiber: 11g | Sugar: 8g | Protein: 18g

Beef and Red Bean Chili

SERVES 6

The depth of flavor in this Beef and Red Bean Chili makes it taste like it was simmering on the stove top all day. Use a food processor to save time by not having to chop the onions, garlic, celery, and jalapeño pepper. Some ideas for quick and easy chili toppings are shredded cheese, sour cream or Greek yogurt, cilantro leaves, pickled jalapeños, tortilla chips, chopped sweet or red onion, and diced avocado.

PREP TIME: 5 MINUTES • ACTIVE COOK TIME: 10 MINUTES • HANDS-OFF COOK TIME: 30 MINUTES

5 cloves garlic, peeled

2 medium celery stalks, roughly chopped into chunks

1 small jalapeño pepper, stem sliced off, roughly chopped into chunks

1 medium yellow onion, peeled and quartered

3½ tablespoons chili powder

1 tablespoon ground cumin

2 teaspoons dried oregano

1½ teaspoons kosher salt

½ teaspoon crushed red pepper flakes

2 dried bay leaves

1 tablespoon avocado oil

1 pound 80% lean ground beef

1 (28-ounce) can crushed tomatoes, including juice

1 (8-ounce) can unsalted tomato sauce

1 cup low-sodium chicken broth

2 (15-ounce) cans kidney beans, rinsed and drained

1 Place garlic, celery, and jalapeño in the bowl of a food processor fitted with the "S" or chopping blade. Process until finely chopped. Add onion and pulse a few times until onion is just chopped (you do not want watery onions for this recipe).

2 In a small bowl, combine chili powder, cumin, oregano, salt, red pepper flakes, and bay leaves. Set aside.

3 Heat a large soup pot over medium-high heat. Once hot, add oil and processed vegetables. Sauté, stirring occasionally, 3–4 minutes until onions just start to become tender.

4 Add ground beef to pot. Cook 4–5 minutes, stirring frequently and breaking up beef with a wooden spoon or spatula, until most of the pink is gone.

5 Add spices and stir to coat. Sauté 45–60 seconds, stirring continuously, until spices are fragrant.

6 Add crushed tomatoes, tomato sauce, and broth to pot. Raise heat to high and bring to a boil.

7 Once boiling, add beans. Partially cover, reduce heat to medium, and continue cooking 30 minutes, stirring occasionally.

8 Remove from heat. Use tongs to remove bay leaves and discard. Serve hot.

PER SERVING
Calories: 360 | Fat: 11g | Sodium: 1,349mg |
Carbohydrates: 36g | Fiber: 13g | Sugar: 8g | Protein: 25g

Tips, Substitutions, Time-Savers, and More

This chili is medium hot in terms of spiciness. If you like it mild, omit the jalapeño and use only $1/8$ teaspoon of crushed red pepper flakes. If you like it very spicy, use two jalapeños and bump up the crushed red pepper flakes to 1 teaspoon.

Tomato Soup with Rice and Spinach

SERVES 6

Transform canned tomatoes, broth, rice, a few spices and aromatics, and fresh baby spinach into a delicious and satisfying vegetarian soup in about 30 minutes. Serve with a drizzle of high-quality olive oil and a sprinkle of grated or shaved Parmesan cheese on top.

PREP TIME: 7 MINUTES ● ACTIVE COOK TIME: 5 MINUTES ● HANDS-OFF COOK TIME: 20 MINUTES

2 tablespoons extra-virgin olive oil

1 large yellow onion, peeled and chopped

2 cloves garlic, peeled and chopped

1 tablespoon kosher salt

1 teaspoon ground cumin

1/2 teaspoon smoked paprika

1/2 teaspoon dried thyme

1/4 teaspoon ground turmeric

1 (28-ounce) can unsalted crushed tomatoes, including juice

1 (15-ounce) can unsalted tomato sauce

4 cups low-sodium vegetable broth

1/2 cup uncooked long-grain white rice, rinsed

2 ounces fresh baby spinach leaves

1. Heat a large soup pot over medium heat. Once hot, add oil, onion, garlic, and spices. Sauté 5 minutes, stirring frequently.

2. Add crushed tomatoes, tomato sauce, and broth to pot. Raise heat to high and bring to a boil.

3. Once boiling, add rice. Cover, reduce heat to medium-low and simmer undisturbed 20 minutes.

4. Stir in spinach, then remove from heat. Serve hot.

PER SERVING
Calories: 188 | Fat: 5g | Sodium: 1,288mg | Carbohydrates: 31g | Fiber: 5g | Sugar: 9g | Protein: 5g

Pressure Cooker Beef Barley Stew

SERVES 8

Let your pressure cooker do most of the work to create a thick and satisfying stew in under an hour. This dish tastes even better the next day and continues to thicken as it sits. Add 1 tablespoon of water to any leftovers before reheating to loosen the stew up a bit.

PREP TIME: 10 MINUTES • ACTIVE COOK TIME: 15 MINUTES • HANDS-OFF COOK TIME: 30 MINUTES

2 tablespoons avocado oil, divided

2 pounds boneless beef chuck roast, cut into 1" cubes

3 teaspoons kosher salt, divided

$1\frac{1}{2}$ teaspoons ground black pepper, divided

2 large yellow onions, peeled and chopped

4 medium carrots, cut into $\frac{1}{4}$" half-moons

2 medium celery stalks, cut into $\frac{1}{4}$" half-moons

8 ounces white mushrooms, thickly sliced

8 cups low-sodium beef broth

1 bay leaf

4 sprigs fresh thyme

$1\frac{1}{2}$ cups uncooked pearled barley, rinsed

1 Set a 6-quart or larger pressure cooker to sauté on high. Add 1 tablespoon oil, half of beef cubes, 1 teaspoon salt, and $\frac{1}{2}$ teaspoon pepper. Sauté 5 minutes, turning once, then remove to a plate. Repeat with remaining 1 tablespoon oil, beef cubes, 1 teaspoon salt, and $\frac{1}{2}$ teaspoon pepper. Set aside.

2 Add onion, carrot, celery, and mushrooms to pressure cooker and sauté 5 minutes, stirring frequently.

3 Add broth, bay leaf, thyme, browned beef cubes, and barley. Place lid on pressure cooker and set to sealed on high pressure for 30 minutes.

Continued ▶

4 When cooking time is up, allow for a 10-minute natural pressure release, then quick-release pressure. Use tongs to carefully remove bay leaf and thyme stems.

5 Add remaining 1 teaspoon salt and $1/2$ teaspoon black pepper and stir to combine. Serve hot.

PER SERVING
Calories: 421 | Fat: 17g | Sodium: 1,051mg | Carbohydrates: 38g | Fiber: 8g | Sugar: 4g | Protein: 30g

Tips, Substitutions, Time-Savers, and More

Save time by buying sliced mushrooms, diced onion, and cubed stew meat. Low-sodium chicken broth can be substituted for beef broth.

Creamy Sausage and Kale Soup

SERVES
6

Save time preparing this savory meal by buying prewashed, trimmed, and shredded or chopped kale at the grocery store. Use your food processor to roughly chop the garlic and onion, and scrub your carrots instead of peeling them. This Creamy Sausage and Kale Soup is wonderful served with a crusty bread and Everyday Simple Dinner Salad (see Chapter 4).

PREP TIME: 10 MINUTES ● ACTIVE COOK TIME: 10 MINUTES ● HANDS-OFF COOK TIME: 10 MINUTES

2 tablespoons extra-virgin olive oil

1 large yellow onion, peeled and chopped

4 cloves garlic, peeled and chopped

1 tablespoon kosher salt

3/4 teaspoon fennel seeds

1/2 teaspoon ground black pepper

1/4 teaspoon crushed red pepper flakes

1 pound bulk uncooked mild Italian sausage

3 medium carrots, cut into 1/8" rounds

2 medium celery stalks, cut into 1/8" half-moons

8 cups low-sodium chicken broth

1 bay leaf

1 (10-ounce) bag shredded kale

1 cup heavy cream

1 Heat a large soup pot over medium heat. Once hot, add oil, onion, garlic, salt, fennel, black pepper, and red pepper flakes. Sauté 5 minutes, stirring frequently.

2 Add Italian sausage and sauté 5 minutes, breaking up sausage with a wooden spoon or spatula, until most of the pink is gone.

3 Add carrots and celery and stir to combine. Pour in broth and bay leaf. Bring to a boil.

4 Once boiling, add kale, cover, and lower to a simmer. Simmer undisturbed 10 minutes.

5 Use tongs to remove and discard bay leaf. Slowly stir in cream. Remove from heat and serve.

PER SERVING
Calories: 509 | Fat: 41g | Sodium: 2,541mg | Carbohydrates: 13g | Fiber: 3g | Sugar: 5g | Protein: 17g

Tips, Substitutions, Time-Savers, and More

For a dairy-free version, omit the heavy cream and substitute one 13.5-ounce can of full-fat coconut milk (shaken well to combine before opening). For a lighter-dairy version, use whole milk or half-and-half instead of heavy cream. Spicy Italian sausage can be substituted for mild sausage to add a bit more of a kick.

Chicken Noodle Soup with Fresh Thyme

SERVES
6

Use shredded rotisserie chicken to make this comforting noodle soup in no time. Fresh thyme adds another layer of flavor. This easy and delicious recipe uses wide egg noodles for that authentic taste and texture.

PREP TIME: 10 MINUTES ● ACTIVE COOK TIME: 5 MINUTES ● HANDS-OFF COOK TIME: 25 MINUTES

2 tablespoons extra-virgin olive oil

1 medium yellow onion, peeled and chopped

3 medium carrots, cut into ¼" rounds

2 medium celery stalks, cut into ¼" half-moons

2 teaspoons kosher salt

1 teaspoon ground black pepper

8 cups low-sodium chicken broth

8 sprigs fresh thyme

½ pound rotisserie chicken meat, shredded

4 ounces uncooked extra-wide egg noodles

1 Heat a large soup pot over medium-high heat. Once hot, add oil, wait 45 seconds and then add onion, carrot, celery, salt, and pepper. Sauté 5 minutes, stirring frequently.

2 Add broth and fresh thyme and bring to a boil.

3 Once boiling, add rotisserie chicken and egg noodles.

4 Cover, reduce heat to medium-low and continue cooking 25 minutes or until noodles are tender and most of the thyme leaves have fallen off the stems.

5 Use tongs to remove the thyme stems and discard before serving.

PER SERVING
Calories: 204 | Fat: 6g | Sodium: 1,687mg | Carbohydrates: 18g | Fiber: 2g | Sugar: 3g | Protein: 17g

Tips, Substitutions, Time-Savers, and More
Serve with soup crackers. For a gluten-free option, look for gluten-free egg pasta.

Cabbage and Sausage Soup

SERVES 8

Made with flavorful Italian sausage, tomatoes, onions, carrots, and plenty of cabbage, this hearty, low-carb soup comes together very quickly. Save time by buying shredded green cabbage, organic carrots that can be scrubbed instead of peeled, and peeled garlic cloves from the convenience vegetables section. Serve with crushed red pepper flakes for a kick of heat. To spice up the whole pot, substitute spicy Italian sausage.

PREP TIME: 8 MINUTES ● ACTIVE COOK TIME: 16 MINUTES ● HANDS-OFF COOK TIME: 20 MINUTES

$1\frac{1}{2}$ tablespoons extra-virgin olive oil

1 large yellow onion, peeled, halved, and thinly sliced

$2\frac{1}{4}$ teaspoons kosher salt, divided

8 turns ($\frac{1}{8}$ teaspoon) freshly ground black pepper plus $\frac{1}{2}$ teaspoon ground black pepper, divided

$1\frac{1}{2}$ pounds bulk uncooked mild Italian sausage

6 cloves garlic, peeled and crushed

4 medium carrots, cut into $\frac{1}{2}$" rounds

2 pounds shredded green cabbage

1 (28-ounce) can unsalted diced tomatoes, including juice

6 cups low-sodium chicken broth

Tips, Substitutions, Time-Savers, and More

This reheats great and can be frozen for up to 6 months in freezer-safe storage containers.

1. Heat a large soup pot over medium heat. Once hot, add oil, onion, $\frac{1}{4}$ teaspoon salt, and eight turns ($\frac{1}{8}$ teaspoon) pepper. Sauté, stirring occasionally, 5 minutes, until onions begin to soften.

2. Add Italian sausage and sauté 5 minutes, breaking up sausage with a wooden spoon or spatula, until most of the pink is gone.

3. Add garlic and carrots and sauté 1 minute, stirring continuously, until garlic is fragrant.

4. Raise heat to medium-high. Add cabbage and remaining 2 teaspoons salt and remaining $\frac{1}{2}$ teaspoon pepper. Stir to combine. Sauté 5 minutes, stirring occasionally, until cabbage begins to wilt.

5. Add tomatoes and broth. Bring to a boil. Once boiling, cover and reduce heat to medium-low. Simmer 20 minutes.

6. Remove from heat and serve.

PER SERVING
Calories: 404 | Fat: 28g | Sodium: 1,766mg | Carbohydrates: 18g | Fiber: 5g | Sugar: 8g | Protein: 17g

Shortcut Wonton Soup with Scallions

SERVES
4

Skip the takeout and make this tasty wonton soup in under 10 minutes instead! For a vegetarian version, substitute vegetable or mushroom broth and vegetable or tofu dumplings in place of chicken. Sliced mushrooms make an excellent addition. If you like spice, serve with sriracha on the side.

PREP TIME: 2 MINUTES ● ACTIVE COOK TIME: 5 MINUTES ● HANDS-OFF COOK TIME: N/A

1 tablespoon toasted sesame oil

1 (2") knob fresh gingerroot, sliced in half through the center

8 cups low-sodium chicken broth

5 tablespoons tamari

1 (12-ounce) package frozen, fully cooked mini chicken wontons

3 tablespoons rice vinegar

2 medium scallions, thinly sliced

1 Heat large soup pot over medium heat. Once hot, add oil and ginger. Sauté 2 minutes.

2 Add broth and tamari, increase heat to high and bring to a boil. Once boiling, add frozen wontons and cook 2–3 minutes until wontons are fully heated through. Remove one wonton and cut in half to test that the insides are fully warmed through.

3 Remove from heat, discard ginger, stir in vinegar and scallions, and serve hot.

PER SERVING
Calories: 206 | Fat: 6g | Sodium: 2,754mg | Carbohydrates: 23g | Fiber: 1g | Sugar: 2g | Protein: 12g

SERVES 2

15-Minute Restaurant-Style Egg Drop Soup

Make authentic-tasting restaurant-style egg drop soup in just under 20 minutes in the comfort of your home. This endlessly versatile soup is great with the addition of quick-cooking vegetables like baby spinach, snow peas, and shredded carrots.

PREP TIME: 1 MINUTE ● ACTIVE COOK TIME: 5 MINUTES ● HANDS-OFF COOK TIME: 12 MINUTES

2 medium scallions, white and green parts separated

1 tablespoon avocado oil

1 (3") knob fresh gingerroot, sliced in half through the center

4 cups low-sodium chicken broth

3 tablespoons tamari

1/2 teaspoon fish sauce

1/2 teaspoon ground cumin

1/2 teaspoon ground ginger

1/2 teaspoon ground white pepper

1/4 teaspoon kosher salt

2 large eggs, beaten

1 tablespoon toasted sesame oil

Tips, Substitutions, Time-Savers, and More

For more texture, add some rinsed canned sliced water chestnuts. Serve with sriracha for a kick of heat.

1 Use the back of a knife to smash the white parts of the scallions. Set aside.

2 Heat a medium soup pot or saucepan over medium heat. Once hot, add avocado oil, scallion whites, and gingerroot. Sauté 2 minutes.

3 Add broth, increase heat to high and bring to a boil. Once boiling, lower heat to medium-low and simmer 12 minutes.

4 Use tongs to remove gingerroot and scallion from broth. Discard.

5 Add tamari, fish sauce, and spices and increase heat to medium-high. As soon as broth is bubbling, slowly pour in eggs, distributing evenly. Allow eggs to set 1 minute, then stir with a fork or chopsticks.

6 Remove from heat and stir in green scallions and sesame oil. Serve hot.

PER SERVING
Calories: 250 | Fat: 18g | Sodium: 3,130mg | Carbohydrates: 5g | Fiber: 1g | Sugar: 1g | Protein: 14g

Quick Taco Soup with Ground Beef

SERVES
6

Everything you love about tacos in a warm bowl of soup, this recipe is ready in just 20 minutes! Serve with some or all of the suggested toppings (see sidebar) or ladle over a baked potato or bowl of steamed rice for an extra-hearty meal.

PREP TIME: 4 MINUTES • ACTIVE COOK TIME: 6 MINUTES • HANDS-OFF COOK TIME: 10 MINUTES

2 tablespoons avocado oil

1 medium yellow onion, peeled and chopped

1 pound 80% lean ground beef

2 tablespoons mild taco seasoning

1 (14.5-ounce) can unsalted diced tomatoes, including juice

1 (15-ounce) can unsalted tomato sauce

2 (15-ounce) cans kidney or pinto beans, rinsed, drained, and half-smashed with a fork

4 cups low-sodium chicken broth

1/2 cup frozen yellow sweet corn kernels

1 Heat a large soup pot over medium-high heat. Once hot, add oil and onion. Sauté 3 minutes.

2 Add ground beef to pot. Cook 3 minutes, stirring frequently and breaking up beef with a wooden spoon or spatula, until most of the pink is gone.

3 Add taco seasoning and stir to coat. Add diced tomatoes, tomato sauce, beans, broth, and corn.

4 Raise heat to high and bring to a boil. Once boiling, reduce heat to a simmer over medium-low heat. Simmer 10 minutes, stirring occasionally.

PER SERVING
Calories: 360 | Fat: 13g | Sodium: 845mg | Carbohydrates: 32g | Fiber: 9g | Sugar: 6g | Protein: 25g

Tips, Substitutions, Time-Savers, and More

Avoid adding salt until the cooking is done and you've tasted the soup to see if it's necessary. Top this dish with shredded cheese, sour cream, chopped cilantro, diced avocado, and/or tortilla chips.

Lasagna Soup with Italian Sausage, Fresh Basil, and Grated Parmesan

SERVES 8

Homemade lasagna is a true labor of love. With this easy lasagna soup, you will get all the flavor and goodness of homemade lasagna but without all the work. Whip up a batch about 30 minutes ahead of time and impress your family with a dinner they will absolutely love.

PREP TIME: 5 MINUTES • ACTIVE COOK TIME: 10 MINUTES • HANDS-OFF COOK TIME: 15 MINUTES

2 tablespoons extra-virgin olive oil

1 large yellow onion, peeled and chopped

6 cloves garlic, peeled and crushed

1 tablespoon Italian seasoning

2 teaspoons kosher salt

½ teaspoon ground black pepper

1 pound bulk uncooked mild Italian sausage

1 (28-ounce) can unsalted crushed tomatoes, including juice

1 (14.5 ounce) can unsalted diced tomatoes, including juice

8 cups low-sodium chicken broth

½ pound uncooked lasagna noodles, broken into small pieces

16 ounces full-fat ricotta cheese

8 tablespoons grated Parmesan cheese

8 teaspoons thinly sliced fresh basil leaves

1. Heat a large soup pot over medium heat. Once hot, add oil, onion, garlic, and spices. Sauté 5 minutes, stirring occasionally.

2. Add sausage to pot and continue cooking 5 minutes, stirring occasionally and breaking up sausage with a wooden spoon or spatula, until most of the pink is gone.

3. Add crushed tomatoes, diced tomatoes, and broth. Raise heat to high and bring to a boil.

4. Once boiling, add lasagna noodles. Reduce heat to medium-low and cook uncovered 15 minutes. Gently stir in ricotta until well incorporated.

5. Serve topped with Parmesan and basil.

PER SERVING
Calories: 532 | Fat: 3g | Sodium: 1,730mg | Carbohydrates: 37g | Fiber: 5g | Sugar: 6g | Protein: 24g

15-Minute White Chicken Chili with Sweet Corn

SERVES 6

This chili is a perfect busy night's dinner. Made with ingredients found in your pantry and freezer, the entire soup comes together and is ready to eat in 15 minutes. Serve with your favorite toppings like shredded cheese, sour cream, chopped cilantro, diced avocado, and tortilla chips. For an even more robust meal, serve over a bed of steamed rice.

PREP TIME: 2 MINUTES • ACTIVE COOK TIME: 3 MINUTES • HANDS-OFF COOK TIME: 10 MINUTES

1 tablespoon avocado oil

1 large yellow onion, peeled and chopped

1 tablespoon ground cumin

1½ teaspoons kosher salt

½ teaspoon dried oregano

8 cups low-sodium chicken broth

2 (12-ounce) jars salsa verde

1 cup frozen yellow sweet corn kernels

2 (15-ounce) cans cannellini beans, rinsed and drained

12 ounces shredded rotisserie chicken

1 Heat a large soup pot over medium-high heat. Once hot, add oil, onion, and spices. Sauté 3 minutes, stirring occasionally.

2 Add remaining ingredients, stir to combine, raise heat to high and bring to a boil.

3 Once boiling, lower heat to medium-low and simmer 10 minutes. Serve hot.

PER SERVING
Calories: 299 | Fat: 4g | Sodium: 2,606mg | Carbohydrates: 36g | Fiber: 10g | Sugar: 9g | Protein: 27g

Tips, Substitutions, Time-Savers, and More
To make a creamy version, whisk in ½ cup heavy cream during the last minute of cooking. Try adding a can of diced chilies for some heat. Pinto beans can be substituted for white beans.

White Bean Soup with Orzo and Parmesan Cheese

SERVES 6

This easy vegetarian soup is excellent served with a drizzle of olive oil, a pinch of crushed red pepper flakes, and a sprinkle of chopped parsley and Parmesan cheese.

PREP TIME: 10 MINUTES • ACTIVE COOK TIME: 15 MINUTES • HANDS-OFF COOK TIME: N/A

2 tablespoons extra-virgin olive oil

3 medium carrots, cut into $1/4$" rounds

2 medium celery stalks, cut into $1/4$" half-moons

1 large yellow onion, peeled and chopped

2 cloves garlic, peeled and crushed

1 tablespoon kosher salt

1 teaspoon ground black pepper

2 teaspoons dried thyme

2 (15-ounce) cans cannellini beans, undrained

6 cups low-sodium vegetable broth

$2/3$ cup uncooked orzo

Juice from $1/2$ large lemon

$1/4$ cup grated Parmesan cheese

1. Heat a large soup pot over medium heat. Once hot, add oil, carrots, celery, onion, garlic, salt, pepper, and thyme. Stir to combine. Sauté 5 minutes, stirring frequently.

2. Add beans with liquid and broth to pot. Bring to a boil over high heat.

3. Once boiling, add orzo. Reduce heat to medium and continue cooking, stirring occasionally, 10 minutes.

4. Remove from heat. Stir in lemon juice and Parmesan. Serve hot.

PER SERVING
Calories: 264 | Fat: 6g | Sodium: 1,863mg | Carbohydrates: 46g | Fiber: 12g | Sugar: 6g | Protein: 12g

Tips, Substitutions, Time-Savers, and More
Crusty bread or crunchy crackers are a perfect pairing for this dish. Freeze for up to 6 months. To reheat, defrost in refrigerator for 24 hours, transfer to a pot with a lid, and warm over a medium-low heat, stirring occasionally, until heated through.

CHAPTER SIX

SAVORY SMALL PLATES AND SIDES

Savory small plates and sides can be made quickly and without a lot of effort. Whether you are getting ready for a big game, family game night, a visit with friends, or a date night in, you will find easy sharing plates in this chapter, like Black Bean Sheet Pan Nachos, Baked Brie with Apricot Jam and Sliced Almonds, and Shortcut Air Fryer Buffalo Chicken Wings with Celery that taste like they came from your favorite sports bar. With just 2 minutes of prep time, you can combine a few easy-to-find ingredients into a slow cooker to make a warm Slow Cooker Creamy Bean and Salsa Dip to serve with tortilla chips or raw peppers. Or use your food processor to "whip" feta cheese into a magical Whipped Feta Dip for fresh vegetables.

The side dish recipes in this chapter include vegetables that naturally need very little prep time and prepared vegetables that will save you massive amounts of time and effort. Use frozen peas to make Frozen Peas with Lemon Butter in about 5 minutes. Whip up Toasted Garlic Couscous with Parsley in under 9 minutes and Parmesan-Crusted Broccoli Florets in about 20 minutes. Simple *and* savory!

Slow Cooker Creamy Bean and Salsa Dip

SERVES
8

This easy slow cooker bean dip takes 2 minutes to get started. Then, set it, forget it, and serve when the cooking time is up. Serve with tortilla chips.

PREP TIME: 2 MINUTES ● ACTIVE COOK TIME: N/A ● HANDS-OFF COOK TIME: 3 HOURS

1 (16-ounce) jar spicy salsa

1 (8-ounce) package cream cheese

1 (15-ounce) can pinto beans, rinsed and drained

1 (15-ounce) can kidney beans, rinsed and drained

1 (15-ounce) bag tortilla chips

1 Combine all ingredients except tortilla chips in a slow cooker. Cover and set to low for 3 hours. Stir every hour to make sure cream cheese is well incorporated.

2 When ready to serve, set slow cooker to warm and place tortilla chips in a bowl next to the slow cooker.

PER SERVING
Calories: 192 | Fat: 9g | Sodium: 682mg | Carbohydrates: 19g | Fiber: 6g | Sugar: 4g | Protein: 7g

Tips, Substitutions, Time-Savers, and More
Raw sweet baby peppers are also a fantastic partner for this dip. They hold up well, add crunch and fiber, and offer a healthy option for those who may want to avoid chips. Leftovers can be transferred to a container with a lid and refrigerated for up to 3 days. Warm in the microwave for 1–2 minutes at medium power until heated through.

Whipped Feta Dip

SERVES
8

Use your food processor to whip up a healthy and flavor-loaded vegetable dip in 5 minutes start to finish (including cleanup time!). This zesty feta cheese–based dip can be made ahead of time and served chilled. It's a fantastic partner for any fresh vegetables like cucumber rounds, carrots, peppers, broccoli, celery, cauliflower, snap peas, and more. For crunch, serve with pita chips.

PREP TIME: 5 MINUTES • ACTIVE COOK TIME: N/A • HANDS-OFF COOK TIME: N/A

8 ounces Greek feta cheese,
broken into chunks

$^3/_4$ cup full-fat plain Greek yogurt

Zest from 1 medium lemon

$^1/_4$ teaspoon kosher salt

3 tablespoons extra-virgin olive
oil, divided

$^1/_2$ teaspoon dried oregano

$^1/_4$ teaspoon crushed red pepper
flakes

1 Add feta, yogurt, lemon zest, and salt to the bowl of a food processer fitted with the "S" or chopping blade.

2 Turn on and slowly drizzle in $2^1/_2$ tablespoons oil while the food processor is running.

3 Use a spatula to transfer mixture to a serving platter and top with remaining $^1/_2$ tablespoon oil, oregano, and red pepper flakes.

PER SERVING
Calories: 140 | Fat: 12g | Sodium: 340mg |
Carbohydrates: 2g | Fiber: 0g | Sugar: 2g |
Protein: 6g

Black Bean Sheet Pan Nachos

Re-create your favorite sports bar appetizer at home in 20 minutes. These easy and endlessly customizable Black Bean Sheet Pan Nachos can be put together in no time and will feed a hungry crowd for the big game or a fun and simple family dinner.

PREP TIME: 8 MINUTES ● ACTIVE COOK TIME: N/A ● HANDS-OFF COOK TIME: 12 MINUTES

1 (16-ounce) bag hearty tortilla chips

1 (15-ounce) can seasoned black beans

4 cups shredded Mexican-style cheese blend

1½ cups pico de gallo

1 cup prepared guacamole

½ cup sour cream

¼ cup pickled jalapeños, drained

2 medium scallions, thinly sliced

1 Preheat oven to 375°F. Line a baking sheet with parchment paper or tinfoil.

2 Arrange half of the chips in a single, slightly overlapping layer on sheet. Top with half of beans, then half of cheese. Repeat layering with remaining chips, beans, and cheese.

3 Bake on the center rack 10–12 minutes until cheese is melted and just beginning to brown. Watch closely near the end so the cheese doesn't burn.

4 Remove baking sheet to a heat-safe surface. Top with pico de gallo, dollops of guacamole, drizzles of sour cream, jalapeños, and scallions. Serve immediately.

PER SERVING
Calories: 840 | Fat: 46g | Sodium: 1,267mg | Carbohydrates: 73g | Fiber: 8g | Sugar: 7g | Protein: 28g

Tips, Substitutions, Time-Savers, and More
No time to make or buy guacamole? Diced avocado is a great substitute. Greek yogurt can be swapped for sour cream, and chopped cilantro leaves are a great stand-in for sliced scallions. Refried black beans are also an excellent addition instead of seasoned canned black beans.

Baked Brie with Apricot Jam and Sliced Almonds

SERVES 8

Whip up a beautiful appetizer in under 25 minutes that will impress your friends and family. Save even more time by preparing the brie wheel with the jam and almonds up to 24 hours in advance and popping it into a preheated oven when ready to serve. Serve with water crackers, crusty bread, and/or sliced apples and pears.

PREP TIME: 4 MINUTES • ACTIVE COOK TIME: N/A • HANDS-OFF COOK TIME: 20 MINUTES

1 (8-ounce) wheel brie cheese
⅓ cup apricot jam
2 tablespoons sliced almonds

1 Preheat oven to 350°F. Line a baking sheet with parchment paper.

2 Place brie on prepared baking sheet and top with jam. Use a knife to evenly spread the jam around the top of the brie wheel from edge to edge.

3 Place the almonds around the edge of the top of the brie, using the jam as "glue" to form a decorative trim.

4 Bake on center rack 16–20 minutes until center is warm and gooey.

5 Allow to cool 5 minutes before serving.

PER SERVING
Calories: 135 | Fat: 8g | Sodium: 183mg |
Carbohydrates: 9g | Fiber: 0g | Sugar: 6g | Protein: 6g

Pressure Cooker Deviled Eggs with Pickled Jalapeños

SERVES
6

The 5:3:5 electric pressure cooker method is foolproof for making perfect hard-cooked eggs every single time. Not only is this method easy and mostly hands-off; the eggs are also much easier to peel thanks to the pressurized cooking environment separating the inner shell lining from the cooked egg.

PREP TIME: 5 MINUTES ● ACTIVE COOK TIME: N/A ● HANDS-OFF COOK TIME: 5 MINUTES

1 cup water
12 large eggs
$1/3$ cup mayonnaise
1 tablespoon yellow mustard
1 tablespoon pickled jalapeño juice
$1/2$ teaspoon kosher salt
$1/4$ teaspoon ground black pepper
24 pickled jalapeño rounds

1. Pour water into a 6-quart or larger pressure cooker. Place short trivet into pressure cooker and carefully place 6 eggs on it. Add taller trivet and place remaining 6 eggs on top. Make sure that the silicone ring insert on the bottom of the lid is properly inserted. Secure the lid to the pot and set for 5 minutes to manual, high pressure.

2. When cooking time is up, set a timer for 3 minutes. Fill a large bowl with ice cubes $2/3$ of the way from the top. Add very cold water until bowl is $3/4$ full.

3. As soon as the timer is up, manually release pressure, remove lid, and use tongs to transfer eggs to ice bath for 5 minutes.

4. Peel eggs and transfer to a cutting board. Use a paring knife to slice each egg in half, gently remove the cooked yolks to a small bowl, and arrange the whites on a serving platter.

Continued ▶

5 Add mayonnaise, mustard, jalapeño juice, salt, and pepper to bowl with egg yolks. Use a fork to mash until well mixed.

6 Spoon mixture into egg white halves. Top each with a pickled jalapeño. Serve.

PER SERVING
Calories: 263 | Fat: 18g | Sodium: 1,929mg |
Carbohydrates: 6g | Fiber: 2g | Sugar: 3g | Protein: 14g

Tips, Substitutions, Time-Savers, and More

You can make the hard-cooked eggs up to 4 days in advance. If your pressure cooker comes with only one stainless steel trivet insert, consider buying a second one of a different height. These can easily be found online or in kitchen supply stores. Cook times can vary depending on the size and model of your pressure cooker.

Skillet Green Beans with Balsamic Vinegar

SERVES 4

Bags of prewashed and trimmed green beans (refrigerated, not frozen) are a versatile powerhouse when it comes to quick meals and sides. For this recipe, you quickly sauté them in a combination of oil and butter with a few spices for approximately 5 minutes. Finish with balsamic vinegar, and you get a delicious and easy side dish that is packed with flavor.

PREP TIME: N/A • ACTIVE COOK TIME: 5 MINUTES • HANDS-OFF COOK TIME: N/A

1 tablespoon extra-virgin olive oil
1 tablespoon salted butter
1 (12-ounce) bag cleaned and trimmed green beans
1/2 teaspoon kosher salt
1/8 teaspoon garlic powder
1/8 teaspoon ground black pepper
1 tablespoon balsamic vinegar

1 Heat a 12" skillet over medium heat. Once hot, add oil and butter, wait 90 seconds and add green beans, salt, garlic powder, and pepper. Toss to combine.

2 Sauté green beans 3 minutes, then add vinegar and continue cooking 1-2 minutes, stirring occasionally, until green beans are just tender. If you prefer the green beans softer, sauté an additional 2 minutes. Serve immediately.

PER SERVING
Calories: 85 | Fat: 6g | Sodium: 319mg |
Carbohydrates: 7g | Fiber: 2g | Sugar: 3g | Protein: 2g

Shortcut Air Fryer Buffalo Chicken Wings with Celery

SERVES
2

Homemade buffalo chicken wings that taste like they came from your favorite pub are possible at home with a few easy shortcuts. Use the air fryer to quickly cook crispy wings and douse them in a simple combination of melted butter and hot sauce or your favorite bottled buffalo sauce to save even more time. Serve with celery and prepared blue cheese dressing (or ranch if you prefer).

PREP TIME: 5 MINUTES ● ACTIVE COOK TIME: N/A ● HANDS-OFF COOK TIME: 20 MINUTES

3 pounds uncooked chicken wing pieces

Nonstick cooking spray

1 teaspoon kosher salt

1/2 teaspoon ground black pepper

6 tablespoons salted butter

3/4 cup Frank's RedHot Original Cayenne Pepper Sauce

8 medium celery stalks, trimmed and cut in half

1/4 cup prepared blue cheese dressing

Tips, Substitutions, Time-Savers, and More

Save even more time by picking up a bag of prewashed celery pieces. Feel free to substitute your favorite bottled buffalo sauce. Look for a sauce that is free of excessive gums, fillers, and hard-to-pronounce ingredients. And don't crowd the air fryer basket, or you won't get crispy wings.

1 Place chicken wing pieces on a baking sheet. Pat dry with a paper towel and then spray with cooking spray.

2 Evenly sprinkle salt and pepper over wings and place into the basket of an air fryer in a single layer.

3 Set air fryer to 400°F for 20 minutes. Flip wings once halfway through cook time.

4 While wings are cooking, melt butter in a large microwave-safe bowl on high 60 seconds. When butter is mostly melted, remove and whisk in hot sauce until well combined. Set aside. (You may need to whisk again right before serving if the mixture separates as the butter cools.)

5 Remove wings from air fryer and toss in sauce. Serve immediately with celery and blue cheese dressing on the side.

PER SERVING
Calories: 1,111 | Fat: 85g | Sodium: 3,033mg | Carbohydrates: 11g | Fiber: 3g | Sugar: 3g | Protein: 61g

Smoky Air Fryer Brussels Sprouts

Save prep time by using whole Brussels sprouts—no cutting necessary. Mix the whole sprouts with simple and flavor-packed spices before tossing them into the basket of the air fryer. Fifteen minutes later, you will be delivered perfectly cooked, smoky Brussels sprouts with crispy, crunchy edges.

PREP TIME: 2 MINUTES • ACTIVE COOK TIME: N/A • HANDS-OFF COOK TIME: 14 MINUTES

1 pound whole Brussels sprouts, ends trimmed

2 tablespoons extra-virgin olive oil

1 teaspoon smoked paprika

1/2 teaspoon kosher salt

1/8 teaspoon ground black pepper

1 Toss Brussels sprouts with oil and spices in a large bowl until well coated. Transfer to the basket of an air fryer in a single layer (a couple doubled up is fine, but the more space you have, the crispier the sprouts will get).

2 Set the air fryer to 390°F for 14 minutes. Shake the basket three times during cooking. Serve immediately.

PER SERVING
Calories: 97 | Fat: 7g | Sodium: 311mg | Carbohydrates: 8g | Fiber: 3g | Sugar: 2g | Protein: 3g

Tips, Substitutions, Time-Savers, and More

No air fryer? Preheat your oven to 450°F. Prepare Brussels sprouts as instructed and spread out on a baking sheet in a single layer. Bake on the center rack 25–30 minutes until centers are tender and outsides are brown and crispy. Add 1/4 teaspoon crushed red pepper flakes along with the smoked paprika, or substitute hot smoked paprika for a spicy kick.

Oven-Roasted Cabbage Wedges

SERVES 4

Cabbage is one of the most affordable and nutritious vegetables available. Transform simple green cabbage into a drool-worthy side dish by letting your oven do most of the work. Cheese lovers, add a teaspoon of grated Parmesan to each cabbage wedge just before serving or melt a bit of shredded Cheddar on top of each wedge for an even cheesier version of this easy recipe.

PREP TIME: 5 MINUTES ● ACTIVE COOK TIME: N/A ● HANDS-OFF COOK TIME: 1 HOUR

1 (3-pound) head green cabbage, sliced into eight wedges

¼ cup extra-virgin olive oil

1 teaspoon kosher salt

½ teaspoon ground black pepper

1 Preheat oven to 400°F.

2 Place cabbage wedges on an ungreased baking sheet and evenly drizzle on all sides with oil. Sprinkle with salt and pepper and place wedges flat-side down on sheet.

3 Bake on the center rack 30 minutes. Carefully flip each wedge to the other flat side and continue roasting 30 minutes or until wedges are brown and edges are crispy. Serve immediately.

PER SERVING
Calories: 187 | Fat: 13g | Sodium: 630mg | Carbohydrates: 16g | Fiber: 7g | Sugar: 9g | Protein: 4g

Parmesan-Crusted Broccoli Florets

SERVES 2

Transform boring broccoli florets into something special by tossing them with olive oil, grated Parmesan cheese, and a few select spices. Want to avoid turning on your oven? You can cook these delicious Parmesan-Crusted Broccoli Florets in an air fryer set to 390°F for 12 minutes. Squeeze a bit of fresh lemon juice over the florets, followed by a sprinkle of grated Parmesan, just before serving.

PREP TIME: 3 MINUTES ● ACTIVE COOK TIME: N/A ● HANDS-OFF COOK TIME: 20 MINUTES

1 (12-ounce) bag fresh broccoli florets

2 tablespoons extra-virgin olive oil

2 tablespoons grated Parmesan cheese

1/2 teaspoon kosher salt

1/4 teaspoon ground black pepper

1/8 teaspoon crushed red pepper flakes

1 Preheat oven to 425°F and line a baking sheet with parchment paper or tinfoil.

2 Combine all ingredients in a large bowl. Transfer to prepared baking sheet and roast 15–20 minutes until broccoli is beginning to brown but is not burnt.

PER SERVING
Calories: 198 | Fat: 14g | Sodium: 1,890mg | Carbohydrates: 12g | Fiber: 4g | Sugar: 3g | Protein: 6g

Toasted Garlic Couscous with Parsley

SERVES 4

Couscous is a magical side dish since it doesn't actually require any cook time. For this Toasted Garlic Couscous with Parsley, you only need to sauté or toast the crushed garlic for about 1 minute, add a few spices, some parsley, and water, and bring to a boil. Add the couscous, turn off the heat, and allow the couscous to work its magic by absorbing all of the flavor.

PREP TIME: 3 MINUTES • ACTIVE COOK TIME: 30 SECONDS • HANDS-OFF COOK TIME: 5 MINUTES

2 tablespoons extra-virgin olive oil

4 cloves garlic, peeled and crushed

1 cup water

1 teaspoon kosher salt

$1/8$ teaspoon crushed red pepper flakes

$1/4$ cup finely chopped flat-leaf parsley, divided

1 cup uncooked plain couscous

1 tablespoon freshly squeezed lemon juice

1 Heat a small saucepan over medium-high heat. Once hot, add oil and garlic. Sauté, stirring constantly, 30 seconds.

2 Add water, increase heat to high and bring to a boil.

3 Once boiling, add salt, red pepper flakes, $1/8$ cup parsley, and couscous. Cover, turn off heat, and let stand undisturbed 5 minutes.

4 Remove cover, use a fork to fluff, and stir in remaining $1/8$ cup parsley and lemon juice. Serve warm.

PER SERVING
Calories: 228 | Fat: 7g | Sodium: 588mg | Carbohydrates: 35g | Fiber: 2g | Sugar: 0g | Protein: 6g

Tips, Substitutions, Time-Savers, and More

Substitute quinoa for couscous to make this gluten-free. Make sure to properly adjust the water ratio (1 cup quinoa to $1 3/4$ cups water) and cooking time, as quinoa needs to cook for close to 20 minutes. Another way to add more flavor is to add the quinoa before the garlic and "toast" the grains for a few minutes in the cooking oil before adding the water.

Pressure Cooker Mashed Yukon Gold Potatoes

SERVES 6

The easiest, mostly hands-off mashed potatoes you will ever make! No peeling, boiling, or straining. The real secret here is using Yukon Gold potatoes: They are naturally very creamy and buttery, and their skins are thin and perfect for mashing when cooked. If you have dried chives on hand, serve with a pinch or two on top for garnish.

PREP TIME: 3 MINUTES • ACTIVE COOK TIME: N/A • HANDS-OFF COOK TIME: 9 MINUTES

2 1/2 pounds unpeeled Yukon Gold potatoes, quartered

1/2 cup water

1 1/2 teaspoons kosher salt, divided

1/2 teaspoon ground black pepper, divided

6 tablespoons salted butter, divided

2 tablespoons whole milk

1 Place potatoes, water, 1 teaspoon salt, 1/4 teaspoon pepper, and 4 tablespoons butter in the insert of a 6-quart or larger pressure cooker.

2 Make sure silicone seal is properly inserted with no gaps and place lid on. Set to high pressure for 9 minutes.

3 When cooking time is up, quick-release pressure. Add remaining 1/2 teaspoon salt, remaining 1/4 teaspoon pepper, remaining 2 tablespoons butter, and milk.

4 Use a large fork or potato masher to mash potatoes and combine ingredients. Serve warm.

Tips, Substitutions, Time-Savers, and More

Any type of plain, unsweetened milk will do the job to loosen up the potatoes. Refrigerate any leftovers for up to 3 days. These mashed potatoes reheat great in the microwave (approximately 60–90 seconds). Freezing is not recommended, as the texture of mashed potatoes changes dramatically in the freezing process and can become grainy or watery when reheated.

PER SERVING
Calories: 250 | Fat: 11g | Sodium: 685mg | Carbohydrates: 33g | Fiber: 4g | Sugar: 2g | Protein: 4g

Frozen Peas with Lemon Butter

SERVES 4

Frozen peas are the star of this simple and flavorful side dish. Combine a bag of frozen peas, butter, and lemon zest and juice for one of the easiest and tastiest quick side dishes you will ever make.

PREP TIME: 2 MINUTES • ACTIVE COOK TIME: 4 MINUTES • HANDS-OFF COOK TIME: N/A

2 tablespoons salted butter

1 (1-pound) bag frozen peas

1 teaspoon kosher salt

1/4 teaspoon ground black pepper

Zest and juice from 1 medium lemon

1 Add butter and frozen peas to a 12" skillet over medium heat. Sauté 1 minute, stirring frequently to melt the butter and heat the peas through.

2 Raise heat to medium-high. Add salt, pepper, lemon zest and juice. Cook 3 minutes, stirring frequently. Serve immediately.

PER SERVING
Calories: 139 | Fat: 6g | Sodium: 749mg | Carbohydrates: 16g | Fiber: 5g | Sugar: 6g | Protein: 6g

CHAPTER SEVEN

DINNERS THAT DON'T TAKE ALL DAY

We are all familiar with the daily grind of figuring out what to feed ourselves and the people around us for dinner. Even for those of us who love to cook, it can be tiring and time-consuming day after day. In this chapter, you will find a collection of easy, whole-food recipes to help you get a delicious dinner on the table in no time.

These dinner recipes are fast, have minimal prep time and cleanup, are cost-effective, and cut down on as many steps as possible without sacrificing taste. And, since it's important that a good dinner include at least one vegetable, these recipes either include vegetables without extra complication or direct you to an Everyday Simple Dinner Salad recipe (see Chapter 4), which takes just 3 minutes to get on the table. You will find a range of cooking techniques from baking in the oven and using an electric pressure cooker, to hands-off cooking in a slow cooker, low-oil crisping in an air fryer, and one pot stove top meals to meet you where you are comfortable—or help you to try a new, easy method that could save you even more time than you thought possible.

Deconstructed California Roll Sushi Bowls with Spicy Sauce

SERVES
4

Sushi rice provides the most authentic flavor and texture, but it's perfectly fine to substitute cooked long-grain white or brown rice. You will find both toasted nori sheets and pickled sushi ginger in the same aisle of the grocery store where you find soy sauce or tamari. For a milder version of sauce, reduce sriracha to 1 teaspoon, taste, and slowly add more until your desired spice level is achieved.

**PREP TIME: 15 MINUTES ● ACTIVE COOK TIME: N/A ●
HANDS-OFF COOK TIME: 5 MINUTES (ACCORDING TO EDAMAME DIRECTIONS)**

½ cup mayonnaise

1 tablespoon sriracha

1 teaspoon tamari

½ teaspoon lime juice

1 cup frozen shelled edamame

2 cups warm prepared sushi rice

1 large avocado, peeled, pitted, and thinly sliced

1 large English cucumber, thinly sliced

8 ounces pasteurized lump crabmeat

4 sheets toasted nori seaweed, thinly sliced

4 tablespoons pickled sushi ginger

1 In a small bowl, combine mayonnaise, sriracha, tamari, and lime juice until well mixed and smooth. Set aside.

2 Cook edamame according to package directions. Drain well. Set aside.

3 Divide rice among four serving bowls. Top each with equal amounts edamame, avocado, cucumber, crabmeat, nori, and ginger. Finish by drizzling sriracha sauce over each bowl and serve immediately.

PER SERVING
Calories: 482 | Fat: 27g | Sodium: 952mg |
Carbohydrates: 38g | Fiber: 6g | Sugar: 4g | Protein: 19g

Tips, Substitutions, Time-Savers, and More

Poached or leftover plain wild Alaskan salmon or cooked shrimp can be substituted for crabmeat. The sriracha sauce can be made up to 48 hours ahead of serving and refrigerated in a covered jar until ready to use. It is recommended to remove the sauce from the refrigerator for at least 30 minutes before serving so it is easier to drizzle.

One Pot Spanish-Style Rice and Beans

SERVES 8

This hearty pot of Spanish-style rice and beans is a delicious and filling vegetarian dinner. You can freeze leftovers in portions and use them as a base for future meals. Try substituting kidney beans or black beans for the pinto beans.

PREP TIME: 5 MINUTES ● ACTIVE COOK TIME: 13 MINUTES ● HANDS-OFF COOK TIME: 30 MINUTES

¼ cup avocado oil

2 cups long-grain white rice, rinsed

1 tablespoon kosher salt

1 tablespoon ground cumin

1 tablespoon chili powder

2 teaspoons dried oregano

1 teaspoon ground black pepper

1 (14.5-ounce) can unsalted diced tomatoes, including juice

1 medium yellow onion, peeled and chopped

4 garlic cloves, peeled and crushed

4 cups low-sodium vegetable broth

1 bay leaf

2 (15-ounce) cans pinto beans, rinsed and drained

Juice of 1 medium lime

1. Heat a large soup pot or Dutch oven over medium heat. Once hot, add oil and rice, stirring to coat.

2. Sauté rice 10 minutes, stirring occasionally, until rice starts to toast and has a golden color.

3. Add spices and stir to combine. Add tomatoes, onion, and garlic. Continue cooking 3 minutes, stirring frequently so rice doesn't burn or stick.

4. Add broth and bay leaf. Stir to combine, raise heat to high and bring to a boil. Once boiling, cover, reduce heat to medium-low, and simmer 12 minutes.

5. Remove cover (do not stir) and add beans in a layer on top of rice. Replace the cover and continue simmering 12 more minutes.

6. Remove from heat (do not stir) and let stand 6 minutes.

7. Remove bay leaf, fluff rice, gently mix in beans, and drizzle with lime juice. Serve.

Tips, Substitutions, Time-Savers, and More

For a richer option, use low-sodium chicken broth and add 2 tablespoons of salted butter in with the broth. To add some heat, add some or all of 1 can of finely chopped chipotles in adobe sauce.

PER SERVING
Calories: 328 | Fat: 7g | Sodium: 1,398mg | Carbohydrates: 54g | Fiber: 6g | Sugar: 2g | Protein: 10g

Red Curry Salmon with Snow Peas

SERVES 4

Use store-bought red curry paste as a shortcut to make this delicious red curry salmon dinner in under 25 minutes. This naturally low-carb meal is loaded with healthy fats, lots of flavor, and a nice serving of snow peas. For a heartier meal, consider serving the curry over a side of jasmine or basmati rice.

PREP TIME: 5 MINUTES • ACTIVE COOK TIME: 18 MINUTES • HANDS-OFF COOK TIME: N/A

3 tablespoons avocado oil, divided

1 pound snow peas

1/4 cup Thai Kitchen Red Curry Paste

1 (13.5-ounce) can full-fat coconut milk, shaken before opening

4 (6-ounce) wild Alaskan salmon fillets

1 teaspoon fish sauce

1/4 teaspoon kosher salt

Juice of 1/2 medium lime

2 medium scallions, thinly sliced

1 Heat a 12" skillet over medium-high heat. Once hot, add 2 tablespoons oil and snow peas. Cook, shaking the pan and stirring constantly to move around the snow peas, 2 minutes. Transfer to a large plate and set aside.

2 Add remaining 1 tablespoon oil to same skillet over medium heat. Heat 30 seconds, then add curry paste. Sauté, stirring continuously, 45 seconds to 1 minute until fragrant.

3 Add coconut milk and whisk until completely dissolved. Keep the heat at medium-high and bring coconut mixture to a boil.

4 Once curry mixture begins to bubble, add salmon fillets skin-side up. Cook 8–10 minutes (depending on thickness of fish), occasionally spooning sauce over fish.

5 Once fish is cooked through, remove fillets and set aside.

Continued ▶

6   Keep heat at medium-high and reduce curry sauce 3–5 minutes, stirring or whisking frequently, until sauce has thickened and clings to a cooking spoon or spatula.

7   Remove from heat and stir in fish sauce, salt, and lime juice.

8   Divide curry sauce over salmon fillets and cooked snow peas on serving plates. Top with scallions. Serve.

PER SERVING
Calories: 561 | Fat: 36g | Sodium: 826mg | Carbohydrates: 15g | Fiber: 4g | Sugar: 5g | Protein: 44g

Delicata Squash Pepperoni Pizza Boats

SERVES 4

Delicata squash are a great vehicle for flavorful ingredients, and they are loaded with fiber. Plus, the skin is thin and, once cooked, 100 percent edible. So, no extra steps scooping cooked squash from a shell or having to worry about anything but devouring this delish and easy dinner! Serve with Everyday Simple Dinner Salad (see Chapter 4).

PREP TIME: 8 MINUTES • ACTIVE COOK TIME: N/A • HANDS-OFF COOK TIME: 49 MINUTES

4 medium delicata squashes, ends trimmed, halved, seeds and guts scooped out and discarded

4 teaspoons extra-virgin olive oil

1 teaspoon kosher salt

1/2 teaspoon ground black pepper

1/2 cup pizza sauce

1 1/2 cups shredded mozzarella cheese

32 small pepperoni rounds

4 teaspoons grated Parmesan cheese

1 teaspoon dried oregano

1 Preheat oven to 350°F.

2 Place prepared squash halves on a baking sheet cut-side up. Drizzle with oil and sprinkle with salt and pepper.

3 Bake on center rack 45 minutes.

4 Remove baking sheet to heat-safe surface. Turn oven to broil on highest setting.

5 Top squash halves with pizza sauce, followed by mozzarella, pepperoni, Parmesan, and oregano.

6 Carefully place baking sheet back into the oven and broil 3–4 minutes until cheese is melted and beginning to brown. Serve hot.

PER SERVING
Calories: 362 | Fat: 12g | Sodium: 1,229mg | Carbohydrates: 46g | Fiber: 9g | Sugar: 18g | Protein: 21g

Honey Mustard–Baked Salmon with Green Beans

SERVES 4

Use a sheet pan to create a salmon and vegetable dinner for four in about 20 minutes. Save time by using prewashed, trimmed green beans (refrigerated, not frozen) and let the quick honey-mustard sauce flavor everything as it cooks. The trick is to start the pan in a cold oven so that the salmon fillets roast slowly, stay tender, and don't release excess albumin from cooking too quickly.

PREP TIME: 3 MINUTES • ACTIVE COOK TIME: N/A • HANDS-OFF COOK TIME: 20 MINUTES

2 tablespoons extra-virgin olive oil

1 1/2 tablespoons Dijon mustard

1 1/2 tablespoons amber honey

1 tablespoon freshly squeezed lemon juice

1 teaspoon dried dill

1 teaspoon kosher salt

1/2 teaspoon ground black pepper

4 cloves garlic, peeled and crushed

4 (6-ounce) wild Alaskan salmon fillets

1 (12-ounce) bag green beans

1 In a small bowl, whisk together oil, mustard, honey, lemon juice, dill, salt, pepper, and garlic until well combined. Set aside.

2 Spray a sheet pan with nonstick cooking spray. Place salmon fillets on pan skin-side down.

3 Arrange green beans around fillets. Spray salmon and beans with a light coating of nonstick cooking spray.

4 Drizzle honey-mustard mixture over salmon, saving a small amount to drizzle over beans.

5 Place baking sheet into cold oven and set to 400°F. Set a timer for 20 minutes.

6 Once timer ends, check that salmon and beans are cooked to your preference and serve immediately.

PER SERVING
Calories: 352 | Fat: 15g | Sodium: 863mg |
Carbohydrates: 14g | Fiber: 2g | Sugar: 9g |
Protein: 40g

Pressure Cooker Frozen Salmon Dinner with Rice

SERVES 2

The perfect meal for two when you forget to defrost something for dinner. Cook frozen salmon fillets with basmati rice and pair with an Everyday Simple Dinner Salad (see Chapter 4) for a hands-off dinner that truly comes together in no time.

PREP TIME: 5 MINUTES • ACTIVE COOK TIME: N/A • HANDS-OFF COOK TIME: 5 MINUTES

1 cup plus 1 tablespoon water

1 cup white basmati rice, rinsed

3/4 teaspoon kosher salt, divided

2 (6-ounce) frozen wild Alaskan salmon fillets

1/4 teaspoon ground black pepper, divided

1 medium lemon, sliced into six rounds

1 In a 6-quart or larger pressure cooker, combine water, rice, and 1/4 teaspoon salt.

2 Place stainless steel insert into pot so that it is above rice. Place salmon fillets on insert. Sprinkle each fillet with remaining salt and 1/8 teaspoon pepper and place three lemon rounds on top of each fillet.

3 Set pressure cooker to manual, high pressure for 5 minutes.

4 Once done, allow for a 2-minute natural pressure release and then quick-release pressure. Serve.

PER SERVING
Calories: 546 | Fat: 8g | Sodium: 1,588mg | Carbohydrates: 70g | Fiber: 2g | Sugar: 0g | Protein: 46g

Tips, Substitutions, Time-Savers, and More
This recipe only works with frozen salmon, as the cook time matches that of white basmati rice. If you use fresh or defrosted salmon, it will be overcooked. Another great salad option to pair with this dish is the 5-Minute Authentic Greek Salad (see Chapter 4).

Baked Cod with Burst Tomatoes and Feta Cheese

SERVES 4

This Mediterranean-inspired baked cod dish combines grape tomatoes, whole garlic cloves, lemon slices, spices, and feta cheese for an easy and tasty dinner that is mostly hands-off. Serve over rice to soak up the sauce and alongside the Everyday Simple Dinner Salad (see Chapter 4) for more vegetables.

PREP TIME: 5 MINUTES ● ACTIVE COOK TIME: N/A ● HANDS-OFF COOK TIME: 23 MINUTES

For Tomatoes

1 pound grape tomatoes

2 tablespoons extra-virgin olive oil

½ teaspoon kosher salt

¼ teaspoon ground black pepper

¼ teaspoon crushed red pepper flakes

¼ teaspoon dried oregano

6 cloves garlic, peeled

1 medium lemon, sliced into four evenly sized rounds

1 Preheat oven to 425°F.

2 *To make Tomatoes*: Combine all ingredients in a 9" × 13" baking dish. Bake on center rack 15 minutes.

For Fish

4 (6-ounce) wild Alaskan cod fillets

1 tablespoon extra-virgin olive oil

¼ teaspoon kosher salt

¼ teaspoon ground black pepper

¼ teaspoon crushed red pepper flakes

4 ounces Greek feta cheese, crumbled

3 *To make Fish*: While Tomatoes are roasting, place fish fillets on a large plate and pat dry with a paper towel to remove excess moisture.

4 Drizzle fish with oil and sprinkle with salt, black pepper, and red pepper flakes. Rub seasoning mixture onto both sides of fillets. Set aside.

Continued ▶

5 Once Tomatoes are done, remove from oven and use a spatula to "burst" or press down on each tomato until flat and juices release.

6 Nestle cod fillets among burst Tomatoes, using a spatula to cover fillets with some of the Tomatoes. Crumble feta over cod.

7 Bake 8 minutes or until cod is just cooked through and flaky. Remove from heat and serve hot.

PER SERVING
Calories: 330 | Fat: 17g | Sodium: 793mg | Carbohydrates: 7g | Fiber: 2g | Sugar: 4g | Protein: 36g

Shrimp and Andouille Sausage Boil with Corn and Red Potatoes

SERVES 4

An easy and impressive dinner that looks much more complicated than it is.
You can substitute fresh corn for the frozen without adjusting the cooking time, although
it's recommended to cut regular-sized fresh corncobs in half. For an extra kick, double the
amount of Old Bay sprinkled on at the end. Serve with melted butter for dipping.

PREP TIME: 5 MINUTE ● ACTIVE COOK TIME: N/A ● HANDS-OFF COOK TIME: 23 MINUTES

12 cups water

1/2 cup apple cider vinegar

1/2 cup plus 2 tablespoons Old Bay seasoning, divided

1 tablespoon kosher salt

10 whole black peppercorns

6 cloves garlic, peeled

2 medium sweet onions, peeled and quartered

8 medium red potatoes, cut in half

4 small frozen corncobs

1 pound smoked, fully cooked andouille sausage, cut into 2" diagonal pieces

1 pound fresh, uncooked, large wild-caught shrimp, in the shells

1 In a large soup or stock pot over high heat, combine water, vinegar, 1/2 cup Old Bay seasoning, salt, peppercorns, garlic, onion, and potatoes. Bring to a boil.

2 Once boiling, lower heat to medium and continue to cook 15 minutes.

3 Add frozen corncobs and sausage pieces. Bring back to a boil and cook 5 minutes.

4 Add shrimp and boil 3 minutes.

5 Once shrimp is cooked through, immediately strain pot through a colander, transfer all cooked items to a serving platter, and top with remaining 2 tablespoons Old Bay seasoning. Serve immediately.

PER SERVING
Calories: 732 | Fat: 20g | Sodium: 3,280mg |
Carbohydrates: 104g | Fiber: 14g | Sugar: 12g |
Protein: 43g

Bow Tie Pasta with Pesto, Peas, and Shrimp

SERVES
6

This four-ingredient meal in a bowl is a complete dinner done in about 15 minutes! You won't dirty any additional pots or pans since you can boil the frozen shrimp and frozen peas right along with the pasta. Strain everything at once and toss with basil pesto. If you like, you can serve topped with crushed red pepper flakes to add some spice.

PREP TIME: 1 MINUTE • ACTIVE COOK TIME: N/A • HANDS-OFF COOK TIME: 15 MINUTES (ACCORDING TO PASTA DIRECTIONS)

1 pound bow tie pasta
1 pound frozen, uncooked, peeled, deveined medium shrimp
1 cup frozen peas
1½ cups basil pesto

1 Bring a large, covered pot of salted water to a boil over high heat.

2 Cook pasta according to package directions plus 1 minute to accommodate for water temperature changes. Add frozen shrimp to pot for last 4 minutes of cooking time. Add frozen peas to pot with pasta and shrimp for last 2 minutes of cooking time.

3 Strain pasta, shrimp, and peas and return to empty pot. Add pesto to pot and toss to combine. Serve.

PER SERVING
Calories: 582 | Fat: 22g | Sodium: 1,450mg | Carbohydrates: 70g | Fiber: 6g | Sugar: 2g | Protein: 26g

Tips, Substitutions, Time-Savers, and More
You can serve this warm or chilled as pasta salad. Some additional serving ideas include adding halved grape tomatoes for color and a pop of freshness, adding the zest of 1 medium lemon to add brightness, and adding 1 (15-ounce) can of any white beans (rinsed and drained) for extra protein and texture.

Cheesy Pesto Chicken Bake with Kale and Rice

SERVES
6

One bite of this cheesy pesto chicken and rice casserole, and you will be hoping there are leftovers! This easy one pot meal is loaded with so much flavor yet takes very little prep work and hands-on cooking time to create. Substitute cubed, trimmed boneless skinless chicken thighs or even ground chicken for the chicken breast.

PREP TIME: 5 MINUTES • ACTIVE COOK TIME: 10 MINUTES • HANDS-OFF COOK TIME: 22 MINUTES

2 tablespoons extra-virgin olive oil

1 1/2 pounds boneless skinless chicken breast, cut into 1" chunks

1 teaspoon kosher salt

1/2 teaspoon ground black pepper

1/4 teaspoon crushed red pepper flakes

2 cups long-grain white rice, rinsed and drained

1 (10-ounce) bag shredded kale

6 cloves garlic, peeled and crushed

1 cup plus 6 tablespoons basil pesto, divided

4 cups low-sodium chicken broth

1 cup shredded mozzarella cheese

1 Heat a large oven-safe pot or Dutch oven with lid over medium-high heat. Once hot, add oil, chicken pieces, salt, black pepper, and red pepper flakes. Cook chicken uncovered and undisturbed 3 minutes.

2 Turn chicken pieces and cook 3 more minutes until chicken starts to brown.

3 Add rice and stir to combine. Add kale and garlic. Stir to combine.

4 Add 1 cup pesto plus broth. Stir until well mixed and continue cooking until kale is wilted and underneath the broth, about 4 minutes.

5 Raise heat to high and bring to a boil. Once boiling, cover, reduce heat to medium-low, and simmer 22 minutes, stirring occasionally so that the top layer of rice gets mixed in and the rice cooks evenly.

6 While chicken and rice mixture is simmering, preheat oven to 450°F.

Continued ▶

7 When rice is done, remove lid and sprinkle mozzarella over casserole. Place in the oven uncovered and bake 6 minutes or until mozzarella is melted and starting to brown.

8 Serve hot with remaining 6 tablespoons pesto drizzled over top.

PER SERVING
Calories: 651 | Fat: 28g | Sodium: 1,477mg | Carbohydrates: 56g | Fiber: 3g | Sugar: 2g | Protein: 43g

Creamy Paprika Chicken Skillet with Spinach and Tomatoes

SERVES 4

Use full-fat canned coconut milk or heavy cream to make this easy and aromatic paprika chicken skillet dinner. Made with sliced onions, grape tomatoes, and spinach for extra texture and nutrition, it's excellent served over rice or cooked pasta.

PREP TIME: 10 MINUTES ● ACTIVE COOK TIME: 20 MINUTES ● HANDS-OFF COOK TIME: N/A

4 (6-ounce) boneless skinless chicken thighs

2 tablespoons mild paprika

1 teaspoon kosher salt

1/2 teaspoon ground black pepper

1/2 teaspoon ground turmeric

1/2 teaspoon garlic powder

1 tablespoon avocado oil

1 cup grape tomatoes

1 medium yellow onion, peeled, halved, and thinly sliced

4 ounces fresh baby spinach leaves

2/3 cup full-fat canned coconut milk (shaken before opened)

1. In a large bowl, combine chicken thighs with paprika, salt, pepper, turmeric, and garlic powder. Set aside.

2. Heat a 12" skillet over medium heat. Once hot, add oil, then chicken thighs in a single layer. Sauté undisturbed 5 minutes.

3. Flip each chicken thigh and cook 5 more minutes.

4. Add tomatoes and onion, toss to coat, and continue cooking 5 minutes until tomatoes are soft enough to easily burst under the weight of a spatula. Smash all tomatoes so the juices release.

5. Add spinach and coconut milk. Continue cooking 5 minutes, mixing well so that spinach wilts, sauce coats everything, and sauce thickens. Remove from heat and serve hot.

Tips, Substitutions, Time-Savers, and More

Swap heavy cream for coconut milk. If using heavy cream, lower the heat to medium-low after you add the cream so the sauce doesn't break as it thickens. For a pop of heat, add 1/4 teaspoon cayenne pepper to the chicken along with the other spices.

PER SERVING
Calories: 348 | Fat: 20g | Sodium: 703mg | Carbohydrates: 9g | Fiber: 3g | Sugar: 3g | Protein: 32g

Three Cheese–Baked Ziti with Chicken Sausage

SERVES
8

Spend 5 minutes assembling this Three Cheese–Baked Ziti with Chicken Sausage and let the oven do the rest. A little over an hour later, not only will your house smell amazing; you will also have a delicious and comforting dinner ready to feed a crowd.

PREP TIME: 5 MINUTES • ACTIVE COOK TIME: N/A • HANDS-OFF COOK TIME: 65 MINUTES

1 pound uncooked ziti

2 (24-ounce) jars marinara sauce

1/2 cup warm water

16 ounces full-fat ricotta cheese

12 ounces fully cooked Italian-style chicken sausages, cut into 1/4" half-moons

2 cups shredded mozzarella cheese

1/2 cup grated Parmesan cheese

1 Preheat oven to 400°F. Spray a 9" × 13" baking dish with nonstick cooking spray.

2 Add uncooked ziti, pasta sauce, water, ricotta, and sausage to prepared baking dish. Use a butter knife to gently stir ingredients together to incorporate. (It's okay if there are some pockets of ricotta that are not fully incorporated.)

3 Top dish evenly with mozzarella, then sprinkle with Parmesan. Tightly cover with tinfoil.

4 Bake on center rack 45 minutes.

5 Carefully remove tinfoil and bake uncovered for 20 more minutes.

6 Remove to a heat-proof surface and allow to cool 10 minutes before serving.

Tips, Substitutions, Time-Savers, and More
Freeze leftovers for up to 6 months in individual portions for future meals. Serve topped with thinly sliced basil leaves and crushed red pepper flakes. Round out the meal with Everyday Simple Dinner Salad (see Chapter 4).

PER SERVING
Calories: 617 | Fat: 28g | Sodium: 1,215mg | Carbohydrates: 56g | Fiber: 3g | Sugar: 8g | Protein: 29g

Sheet Pan Unbreaded Chicken Parmesan with Roasted Cauliflower

SERVES
4

Traditional chicken parmesan has a crispy, crunchy breading with melted mozzarella on top of the sauce. But when time is short or you just don't feel like cooking, this easy shortcut delivers the familiar flavor you are looking for without a lot of effort. You can find the cauliflower florets in the refrigerated convenience vegetables section of the grocery store. Serve with a side of pasta, rice, or a crusty baguette.

PREP TIME: 6 MINUTES • ACTIVE COOK TIME: N/A • HANDS-OFF COOK TIME: 33 MINUTES

4 (6-ounce) boneless skinless chicken thighs

1 (16-ounce) bag cauliflower florets (not frozen)

2 tablespoons extra-virgin olive oil

1 teaspoon kosher salt

1/2 teaspoon ground black pepper

1/2 teaspoon Italian seasoning

1 cup marinara sauce

1 cup shredded mozzarella cheese

2 tablespoons grated Parmesan cheese

Tips, Substitutions, Time-Savers, and More

If you prefer your melted cheese brown and bubbly, turn on the broiler to the highest setting for the last 2–3 minutes of cheese melting time. When it comes to buying jarred sauce, look for brands that have only a handful of familiar ingredients. Some recommended brands are Rao's Homemade, Monte Bene, and Organico Bello.

1 Preheat oven to 450°F.

2 Place chicken thighs and cauliflower florets onto a sheet pan. Drizzle with oil and sprinkle with salt, pepper, and Italian seasoning. Use your hands to toss until well coated.

3 Bake on center rack 25 minutes. Use a spatula to flip chicken and cauliflower once halfway through cooking time.

4 Remove baking sheet to a heat-safe surface. Use spatula to separate each chicken thigh into a section of the baking sheet with 1/4 of cooked cauliflower.

5 Divide pasta sauce onto each chicken thigh and cauliflower section. Top with mozzarella and Parmesan.

6 Place baking sheet back into oven and bake 6–8 minutes until cheese is completely melted. Remove from heat and serve hot.

PER SERVING
Calories: 421 | Fat: 23g | Sodium: 1,107mg | Carbohydrates: 11g | Fiber: 3g | Sugar: 5g | Protein: 38g

Rotisserie Chicken Fried Rice with Frozen Vegetables

SERVES 4

The secret to good fried rice is using leftover or precooked rice. To make fried rice a quick and easy meal ideal for busy nights, this recipe uses rice, rotisserie chicken, frozen mixed vegetables, and a few seasonings.

PREP TIME: 4 MINUTES • ACTIVE COOK TIME: 8 MINUTES • HANDS-OFF COOK TIME: N/A

1 tablespoon avocado oil

1 (10-ounce) bag frozen mixed vegetables (like peas, carrots, onion)

1/4 cup frozen peas

12 ounces cooked and cooled white rice

8 ounces shredded rotisserie chicken

2 1/2 tablespoons tamari

1/4 teaspoon ground black pepper

1 tablespoon toasted sesame oil

1 Heat a wok or 12" skillet over high heat. Once hot, add avocado oil, mixed vegetables, and peas. Cook 4 minutes, stirring frequently to defrost the vegetables and allow any water to evaporate.

2 Add rice, chicken, tamari, and pepper. Continue cooking 4 minutes, tossing pan and stirring to mix ingredients together.

3 Remove from heat, drizzle with sesame oil, and serve hot.

PER SERVING
Calories: 313 | Fat: 8g | Sodium: 847mg | Carbohydrates: 36g | Fiber: 4g | Sugar: 1g | Protein: 22g

Tips, Substitutions, Time-Savers, and More

Use this recipe as a base template for whatever leftover proteins or vegetables you have on hand. To add a kick of heat, serve with a drizzle of sriracha.

Chicken Bruschetta with Balsamic Drizzle

Traditional tomato bruschetta topping is usually made by dicing plum tomatoes and tossing with chopped onion, basil, olive oil, balsamic, and spices. Here, you save time by skipping the onion and using cherry tomatoes that are simply sliced in half. To save even more time, use rotisserie chicken in place of the chicken breasts.

PREP TIME: 10 MINUTES ● ACTIVE COOK TIME: 20 MINUTES ● HANDS-OFF COOK TIME: N/A MINUTES

For Chicken

4 (6-ounce) boneless skinless chicken breasts

2 tablespoons extra-virgin olive oil, divided

1 teaspoon Italian seasoning

1/2 teaspoon kosher salt

1/4 teaspoon ground black pepper

1/8 teaspoon crushed red pepper flakes

1 *To make Chicken*: In a large mixing bowl, add chicken breasts, 1 tablespoon oil, Italian seasoning, salt, black pepper, and red pepper flakes. Toss until chicken is well coated.

2 Heat a 12" skillet over medium heat. Once hot, add remaining 1 tablespoon olive oil and seasoned chicken to skillet. Sauté undisturbed 10 minutes.

3 Flip chicken and cook 8–10 more minutes until an internal temperature of 165°F is reached.

For Bruschetta

1 pound cherry tomatoes, halved

10 fresh basil leaves, rolled and thinly sliced

2 tablespoons extra-virgin olive oil

1 tablespoon balsamic vinegar

1/2 teaspoon kosher salt

1/8 teaspoon ground black pepper

4 *To make Bruschetta*: Combine tomatoes, basil, oil, vinegar, salt, and pepper in a medium bowl. Set aside.

Continued ▶

For Serving

1 batch Everyday Simple Dinner Salad (see Chapter 4)

4 teaspoons grated Parmesan cheese

4 teaspoons balsamic vinegar

5   Slice Chicken into strips. Divide onto four serving plates over Everyday Simple Dinner Salad. Top each serving with 1/4 Bruschetta (including juice), Parmesan, and balsamic vinegar.

PER SERVING
Calories: 401 | Fat: 33g | Sodium: 857mg |
Carbohydrates: 9g | Fiber: 2g | Sugar: 5g |
Protein: 41g

Tips, Substitutions, Time-Savers, and More

Feel free to follow your favorite cooking method (grilled, air fryer, baked, etc.) for the chicken, but note that this dish is best with warm chicken. If you have leftover chicken, you can warm it up before plating. You can also substitute boneless chicken thighs, shrimp, or your favorite fish—just be sure to modify the cooking time as needed.

The Easiest Teriyaki Chicken with Snap Peas

SERVES
4

This endlessly customizable teriyaki chicken recipe will quickly become a household dinner staple. Whip it up in about 20 minutes for an easy and delicious meal that the whole family will love. To add some heat, add 1 teaspoon of sriracha to the sauce mixture or serve with a drizzle of sriracha. Serve alongside steamed rice.

PREP TIME: 8 MINUTES ● ACTIVE COOK TIME: 13 MINUTES ● HANDS-OFF COOK TIME: N/A

1/4 cup tamari

2 tablespoons granulated sugar

1 tablespoon toasted sesame oil

2 teaspoons arrowroot starch

1 teaspoon sesame seeds

1 teaspoon grated gingerroot

3 cloves garlic, peeled and crushed

2 tablespoons avocado oil

1 1/2 pounds boneless skinless chicken thighs, cut into 1/2" strips

12 ounces snap peas

1 Combine tamari, sugar, sesame oil, starch, sesame seeds, gingerroot, and garlic in a small bowl or measuring cup and set aside.

2 Heat a 12" skillet over medium-high heat. Once hot, add avocado oil and chicken strips. Cook chicken undisturbed 6 minutes.

3 Flip chicken and cook 4 more minutes.

4 Add peas to skillet along with teriyaki sauce. Stir to combine and continue cooking 2–3 minutes until sauce slightly thickens and snap peas are cooked but still crunchy. Remove from heat and serve hot.

PER SERVING
Calories: 384 | Fat: 20g | Sodium: 1,106mg | Carbohydrates: 15g | Fiber: 3g | Sugar: 9g | Protein: 34g

Tips, Substitutions, Time-Savers, and More
Some substitutions that work for this recipe: 3 tablespoons of coconut sugar in place of 2 tablespoons granulated sugar; equal amount of cornstarch for arrowroot starch; sliced boneless skinless chicken breast, sliced pork, sliced beef, cubed baked tofu, or peeled and deveined shrimp in place of chicken thighs.

Leftover Chicken Enchilada Casserole with Corn

Use any kind of leftover cubed or shredded chicken to make this easy one dish meal in a little over a half an hour. Instead of rolling the enchiladas, save time by creating a quick layered casserole in minutes. Top with a drizzle of sour cream or Greek yogurt, a sprinkle of chopped cilantro or sliced scallions, and serve with some diced avocado or guacamole.

PREP TIME: 8 MINUTES • ACTIVE COOK TIME: N/A • HANDS-OFF COOK TIME: 25 MINUTES

1 (15-ounce) jar enchilada sauce

6 (4$\frac{1}{2}$") corn tortillas

12 ounces cooked chicken, shredded or cubed

$\frac{1}{2}$ cup frozen yellow sweet corn kernels

12 ounces shredded Mexican-style cheese

1 Preheat oven to 375°F. In a 9" square casserole dish, spread $\frac{1}{4}$ enchilada sauce.

2 Layer 2 tortillas side by side on top of sauce, then layer with half of chicken, half of corn, $\frac{1}{3}$ shredded cheese, and $\frac{1}{4}$ more enchilada sauce. Repeat to create a second layer.

3 To finish, top casserole with remaining 2 tortillas, remaining enchilada sauce, and remaining cheese.

4 Bake uncovered 25 minutes.

5 Allow to rest 5–10 minutes before serving.

PER SERVING
Calories: 549 | Fat: 25g | Sodium: 1,281mg | Carbohydrates: 24g | Fiber: 4g | Sugar: 9g | Protein: 50g

Horseradish and Dijon Burgers

SERVES 4

Make delicious and flavorful burgers in under 15 minutes with hardly any prep work. Just add horseradish, Dijon mustard, salt, pepper, and parsley. Serve on buns with your favorite toppings, or as lettuce wraps, atop a salad, or as a low-carb burger platter.

PREP TIME: 5 MINUTES ● ACTIVE COOK TIME: 8 MINUTES ● HANDS-OFF COOK TIME: N/A

1 pound 80% lean ground beef
1/4 cup prepared horseradish
1 tablespoon Dijon mustard
1 teaspoon kosher salt
1/2 teaspoon ground black pepper
1/2 teaspoon dried parsley
4 hamburger buns
1 large beefsteak tomato, cut into four thick slices
4 thin slices peeled sweet onion
4 leaves iceberg lettuce

1 In a large bowl, combine ground beef, horseradish, mustard, salt, pepper, and parsley until just mixed. You do not want to overwork ground beef, as it can become tough. Divide mixture into four evenly sized patties.

2 Heat a 12" skillet over medium-high heat. Once hot, add burgers with a bit of space around each one for even browning. Cook 4 minutes per side for medium burgers, turning only once when the burger naturally releases from the pan.

3 Remove from heat. Serve on buns, and topped with tomato, onion, and lettuce.

PER SERVING
Calories: 371 | Fat: 13g | Sodium: 959mg | Carbohydrates: 30g | Fiber: 5g | Sugar: 6g | Protein: 26g

Tips, Substitutions, Time-Savers, and More

You can make the burger patties in advance and refrigerate them for up to 24 hours before cooking. These cook like any other burgers, so feel free to grill, air-fry, bake, broil, or use any other cooking method you like to use for cooking burgers. For medium well, cook for 5 minutes per side. For well done, cook 6 minutes per side.

Philly Cheesesteak–Stuffed Bell Pepper Halves

SERVES 4

This low-carb twist on traditional Philly cheesesteaks is an easy weeknight dinner that the whole family will love. Save time by using ground beef instead of the usual shaved beef sirloin. While provolone is recommended, you can substitute white American cheese or even Cheez Whiz to get that authentic Philly flavor at home!

PREP TIME: 5 MINUTES • ACTIVE COOK TIME: 16 MINUTES • HANDS-OFF COOK TIME: 28 MINUTES

4 medium green bell peppers, halved from stem to root, seeds and ribs removed

2 tablespoons avocado oil

1 extra-large yellow onion, peeled, quartered, and thinly sliced

2 teaspoons kosher salt, divided

2 teaspoons ground black pepper, divided

1 pound 80% lean ground beef

16 slices provolone cheese

1 Preheat oven to 425°F.

2 Place bell pepper halves on an ungreased baking sheet (cut-side up) and spray with nonstick cooking spray. Bake 20 minutes.

3 While peppers are baking, set a 12" skillet over medium heat. Once hot, add oil, onion, and 1 teaspoon each of salt and pepper. Sauté, stirring occasionally, 8 minutes.

4 Add ground beef and remaining 1 teaspoon each of salt and pepper to skillet. Cook 8 minutes, stirring frequently and breaking up beef with a wooden spoon or spatula, until most of the pink is gone.

5 Remove from heat and set aside.

6 Once peppers are done, remove from oven and use a slotted spoon to evenly stuff with meat and onion mixture. Top each pepper half with 2 slices provolone.

Continued ▶

7 Return peppers to oven and cook 5 minutes.

8 Turn oven to broil on highest setting and broil 3 minutes or until cheese is bubbly and beginning to brown. Remove from oven and serve.

PER SERVING
Calories: 707 | Fat: 47g | Sodium: 2,229mg | Carbohydrates: 12g | Fiber: 3g | Sugar: 5g | Protein: 51g

Ground Meat Stir-Fry with Green Beans

SERVES 4

Combine ground turkey with greens beans for a delicious stir-fry dinner that is on the table in 10 minutes—no chopping necessary! This dish is excellent served with leftover or reheated frozen rice. While this recipe uses dark-meat ground turkey, any ground meat will work great.

PREP TIME: 1 MINUTE • ACTIVE COOK TIME: 10 MINUTES • HANDS-OFF COOK TIME: N/A

¼ cup low-sodium tamari

1 teaspoon sriracha

½ teaspoon ground ginger

⅛ teaspoon ground white pepper

1 tablespoon avocado oil

1 pound dark-meat ground turkey

1 (12-ounce) bag prewashed, trimmed string beans (refrigerated, not frozen)

1 tablespoon toasted sesame oil

1 In a small cup, combine tamari, sriracha, ginger, and pepper. Set aside.

2 Heat a 12" or larger skillet or wok over medium-high heat until just starting to smoke. Add avocado oil and ground turkey. Use a wooden spoon or spatula to break up ground meat into small chunks and let cook undisturbed 3 minutes.

3 Stir turkey and sauté 3–4 minutes until most of the pink is gone.

4 Add tamari mixture to turkey, along with beans. Toss until well coated.

5 Place lid on skillet or wok and continue cooking 3 minutes until beans are just tender. If you like your green beans a little softer, cook for 2 more minutes.

6 Remove from heat, drizzle with sesame oil, toss to coat, and serve.

PER SERVING
Calories: 323 | Fat: 20g | Sodium: 812mg |
Carbohydrates: 7g | Fiber: 2g | Sugar: 3g | Protein: 25g

Korean-Inspired Beef and Rice Bowls with Cucumbers and Kimchi

SERVES
4

Combine a simple yet flavor-packed Korean-inspired sauce, ground beef, rice, sliced cucumber, store-bought kimchi, and scallions for a fast and tasty meal that everyone will think is better than takeout. Save time by reheating leftover or frozen rice. If you are feeling extra fancy, sprinkle some toasted sesame seeds on top of the ground beef right before serving.

PREP TIME: 5 MINUTES ● ACTIVE COOK TIME: 10 MINUTES ● HANDS-OFF COOK TIME: N/A

For Sauce

¼ cup tamari

2 tablespoons granulated sugar

1 tablespoon toasted sesame oil

1 tablespoon sesame seeds

1 tablespoon rice vinegar

1 teaspoon ground ginger

⅛ teaspoon ground black pepper

4 cloves garlic, peeled and crushed

1 *To make Sauce:* In a small bowl or measuring cup, combine all ingredients. Set aside.

For Beef

1 tablespoon avocado oil

1½ pounds 80% lean ground beef

3 cups cooked white rice, reheated

1 cup store-bought kimchi

1 large English cucumber, cut into ⅛" half-moons

2 medium scallions, thinly sliced

2 *To make Beef:* Heat a 12" skillet over medium-high heat. Once hot, add oil and ground beef. Sauté 5 minutes, stirring frequently and breaking up beef with a wooden spoon or spatula, until most of the pink is gone.

Continued ▶

3 Pour Sauce over Beef and continue cooking 5 minutes, stirring occasionally, until Sauce is thickened and meat is cooked through.

4 Remove from stove top. Divide rice, beef, kimchi, cucumber, and scallions into four bowls and serve.

PER SERVING
Calories: 645 | Fat: 24g | Sodium: 1,591mg | Carbohydrates: 62g
| Fiber: 3g | Sugar: 12g | Protein: 37g

3-Ingredient Pesto Meatballs

SERVES
4

Take the prep time out of making savory, flavorful meatballs by folding
in prepared pesto and an egg. Just roll, panfry, simmer, and serve. These 3-Ingredient
Pesto Meatballs are excellent simmered in jarred pasta sauce and served over your
favorite pasta, on an Italian roll topped with shredded mozzarella or provolone, or
alongside some reheated rice and Everyday Simple Dinner Salad (see Chapter 4).

PREP TIME: 5 MINUTES • ACTIVE COOK TIME: 6 MINUTES • HANDS-OFF COOK TIME: 20 MINUTES

1 pound 80% lean ground beef
1 large egg
1/2 cup basil pesto
2 teaspoons extra-virgin olive oil
1 (24-ounce) jar marinara sauce

1 Combine ground beef, egg, and pesto in a
large bowl.

2 Separate mixture into four sections in bowl.
Divide each section into quarters and roll each
into a ball for a total of sixteen meatballs.

3 Heat a 12" skillet over medium-high heat. Once
hot, add oil and then meatballs in a single layer
with some room around each one to make it
easy to turn them.

4 Panfry 2–3 minutes per side until browned.
(Use tongs to gently push meatballs over, as
they can break easily.)

5 Transfer meatballs to a medium pot with pasta
sauce and simmer covered 15–20 minutes until
meatballs are completely cooked through.

PER SERVING
Calories: 480 | Fat: 33g | Sodium: 958mg |
Carbohydrates: 11g | Fiber: 2g | Sugar: 5g | Protein: 26g

Ground Pork Egg Roll Bowls

SERVES 4

These easy Ground Pork Egg Roll Bowls are the quick answer when you are craving the flavor of an egg roll but want a healthier option. To add a bit of heat, drizzle with sriracha right before serving. For a heartier meal, serve over a bed of steamed rice. Ground beef or ground turkey can be substituted for ground pork. Black pepper can be substituted for the white pepper.

PREP TIME: 7 MINUTES ● ACTIVE COOK TIME: 13 MINUTES ● HANDS-OFF COOK TIME: N/A

¼ cup tamari

2 tablespoons toasted sesame oil

¼ teaspoon ground white pepper

2 medium scallions, thinly sliced

2 cloves garlic, peeled and crushed

1 tablespoon avocado oil

1 pound ground pork

1 medium yellow onion, peeled, halved, and thinly sliced

1 pound shredded green cabbage

1 cup shredded carrots

1 In a measuring cup or small bowl, combine tamari, sesame oil, pepper, scallions, and garlic. Set aside.

2 Heat a wok or extra-wide (14" or larger) frying pan over medium-high heat. Once hot, add avocado oil and pork. Sauté pork undisturbed 4 minutes to develop a crust on the bottom. Toss pork to break up any large pieces and cook 4 more minutes.

3 Add onion, toss to combine, and cook 2 more minutes.

4 Add cabbage, carrot, and sauce. Cook, stirring frequently to incorporate the meat and vegetables with the sauce, 3 minutes. Serve hot.

PER SERVING
Calories: 385 | Fat: 26g | Sodium: 1,114mg | Carbohydrates: 14g | Fiber: 4g | Sugar: 7g | Protein: 25g

Pressure Cooker Pulled Pork

SERVES
6

Use your pressure cooker to make tender pulled pork with mostly hands-off cook time. This pork is delicious in sandwiches, salads, tacos, burritos, enchiladas, and more. To turn pulled pork into carnitas, spread out pork on a baking sheet and pour ½ cup of juices leftover from the pressure-cooked pork over it. Pop into an oven preheated to 450°F and bake for 15 minutes until edges are browned.

PREP TIME: 5 MINUTES • ACTIVE COOK TIME: 12 MINUTES • HANDS-OFF COOK TIME: 35 MINUTES

3 tablespoons chili powder

2 tablespoons kosher salt

1 tablespoon ground cumin

2 teaspoons dried oregano

½ teaspoon crushed red pepper flakes

⅛ teaspoon ground cloves

1 (6-pound) boneless Boston pork butt roast, cut into chunks

2 tablespoons avocado oil, divided

1 cup low-sodium chicken broth

1 bay leaf

Tips, Substitutions, Time-Savers, and More

To cook this recipe in a slow cooker, sear the pork on the stove top and then transfer to the slow cooker with broth and bay leaf. Set to low for 8 hours or high for 4 hours.

1 In a small bowl, combine spices. Rub all over pork chunks until well coated and all spice mix is used up.

2 Set 6-quart or larger pressure cooker to sauté on high. Once hot, add 1 tablespoon oil and half of pork chunks. Sear 3 minutes per side.

3 Remove seared pork from heat and repeat cooking with remaining 1 tablespoon oil and remaining half of pork.

4 Add all seared pork, broth, and bay leaf back to pressure cooker. Set pressure cooker to manual high pressure for 35 minutes.

5 Once done, allow for a 15-minute natural pressure release and then quick-release pressure.

6 Remove cooked pork to a cutting board and use two large forks to shred.

PER SERVING
Calories: 747 | Fat: 42g | Sodium: 2,714mg |
Carbohydrates: 3g | Fiber: 2g | Sugar: 0g | Protein: 79g

Pulled Pork Street Tacos

Use up leftover pulled pork to make delicious pork street tacos in 15 minutes! Save even more time by skipping the diced avocado and picking up prepared guacamole. For heat, add pickled jalapeños or sprinkle each taco with your favorite spicy hot sauce.

PREP TIME: 15 MINUTES ● ACTIVE COOK TIME: N/A ● HANDS-OFF COOK TIME: N/A

12 ($4^{1}/_{2}$") corn tortillas, warmed

$1^{1}/_{2}$ pounds Pressure Cooker Pulled Pork, warmed

1 (10-ounce) bag shredded green cabbage

2 large avocados, peeled, pitted, and sliced

4 medium radishes, thinly sliced

1 (16-ounce) container pico de gallo

3 medium limes, quartered

Spread out the warmed tortillas on a baking sheet or cutting board. Divide pulled pork, cabbage, avocado, radishes, and pico de gallo among tortillas. Give each a squeeze of fresh lime juice and serve immediately.

PER SERVING
Calories: 550 | Fat: 17g | Sodium: 1,704mg | Carbohydrates: 73g | Fiber: 11g | Sugar: 36g | Protein: 27g

Barbecue Pulled Pork Sandwiches with Shredded Cabbage

SERVES 4

Transform leftover pulled pork into Kansas City–style barbecue pulled pork with just two additional ingredients. Serve on toasted buns with shredded cabbage or coleslaw mix for crunch and balance. Cheese lovers, add a slice or two of Cheddar or pepper jack on top of the pulled pork. For extra heat, add some pickled jalapeños or kick it up with spicy barbecue sauce.

PREP TIME: 5 MINUTES • ACTIVE COOK TIME: 5 MINUTES • HANDS-OFF COOK TIME: N/A

1½ pounds Pressure Cooker Pulled Pork plus ¼ cup cooking liquid

1 cup Kansas City–style barbecue sauce

4 seeded hamburger buns, toasted

1 (10-ounce) bag shredded green cabbage

1 In a medium saucepan, combine pork, its cooking liquid, and barbecue sauce. Heat over medium-low until warmed through, 4–5 minutes.

2 Place bun bottoms on serving plates and layer cabbage evenly on top.

3 Add pork on top of cabbage. Top with bun tops and serve immediately.

PER SERVING
Calories: 814 | Fat: 33g | Sodium: 2,878mg | Carbohydrates: 57g | Fiber: 6g | Sugar: 31g | Protein: 65g

Boneless Taco-Seasoned Pork Chops with Pico de Gallo and Avocado

SERVES 4

Season pork chops with premixed taco seasoning, top with store-bought pico de gallo and diced avocado, and you have a flavorful and nutritious dinner on the table in about 20 minutes. Save time by using two 12" skillets to cook all four pork chops at the same time. Serve with Everyday Simple Dinner Salad (see Chapter 4) and tortilla chips.

PREP TIME: 2 MINUTES • ACTIVE COOK TIME: 20 MINUTES • HANDS-OFF COOK TIME: N/A

4 (6-ounce, 1"-thick) boneless pork chops

4 teaspoons mild taco seasoning

2 tablespoons avocado oil, divided

1 cup pico de gallo

2 medium avocados, peeled, pitted, and diced

Tips, Substitutions, Time-Savers, and More

Pork chops should be cooked to a minimum internal temperature of 145°F:
Medium Rare: 145°F–150°F
Medium: 150°F–155°F
Medium Well: 155°F–160°F
Well Done: 160°F (not recommended, as pork chops can become dry if overcooked)

1 Pat pork chops dry with a paper towel. Sprinkle taco seasoning on each side of pork chops, using your fingers to spread it around.

2 Heat a 12" skillet over medium-high heat. Once hot, add 1 tablespoon oil and 2 pork chops. Sear 5 minutes.

3 Flip pork chops, reduce heat to medium, and continue cooking 5 more minutes.

4 Remove cooked pork chops from skillet and repeat cooking with remaining 1 tablespoon oil and remaining 2 pork chops.

5 Transfer cooked pork chops to a cutting board and let rest 5 minutes. Serve topped with pico de gallo and avocado.

PER SERVING
Calories: 422 | Fat: 22g | Sodium: 633mg | Carbohydrates: 14g | Fiber: 5g | Sugar: 5g | Protein: 42g

Fusilli Pasta with Italian Sausage, Ricotta, and Baby Spinach

SERVES 6

Turn weeknight pasta into something special without adding any extra work or chopping. Freeze any leftovers in individual portions for a quick-reheat lunch later in the week. Serve alongside Everyday Simple Dinner Salad (see Chapter 4) and topped with crushed red pepper flakes and grated Parmesan cheese.

PREP TIME: 2 MINUTES • ACTIVE COOK TIME: 8 MINUTES • HANDS-OFF COOK TIME: 10 MINUTES (ACCORDING TO PASTA DIRECTIONS)

1 pound fusilli

2 tablespoons extra-virgin olive oil

1 pound bulk uncooked mild Italian sausage

6 ounces fresh baby spinach leaves

2 cloves garlic, peeled and crushed

1 (24-ounce) jar marinara sauce

8 ounces ricotta cheese

1 Set a large soup pot of salted water to boil over high heat.

2 While water is heating, heat a Dutch oven or large pot over medium-high heat. Once hot, add oil and sausage. Cook, stirring frequently, 6 minutes, breaking up sausage with a wooden spoon or spatula, until most of the pink is gone.

3 Add spinach and garlic. Continue cooking 2 minutes.

4 Add pasta sauce and ricotta and stir until well combined. Cover and reduce heat to low while pasta cooks, about 10 minutes.

5 Once water is boiling, cook pasta according to package directions. Right before straining, use a measuring cup to scoop out 1/4 cup cooking liquid and pour it into ricotta-sausage mixture.

6 Transfer drained pasta into pot with sauce mixture, toss to combine, and serve hot.

PER SERVING
Calories: 758 | Fat: 39g | Sodium: 1,232mg | Carbohydrates: 66g | Fiber: 5g | Sugar: 5g | Protein: 29g

Herb-Rubbed Bone-In Air Fryer Pork Chops

SERVES 4

Cook bone-in pork chops in the air fryer to avoid turning on the oven or having to clean oil splatter from the stove top. This hands-off recipe is made with a simple dried spice and oil mix from ingredients you have in your pantry. You can make the spice mix right before cooking or marinate the pork chops for up to 24 hours before cooking.

PREP TIME: 5 MINUTES • ACTIVE COOK TIME: N/A • HANDS-OFF COOK TIME: 11 MINUTES

2 tablespoons extra-virgin olive oil

1 tablespoon dried parsley

1 teaspoon kosher salt

1/2 teaspoon ground black pepper

1/2 teaspoon ground cumin

1/2 teaspoon paprika

1/2 teaspoon garlic powder

1/2 teaspoon dried thyme

4 (6-ounce) 1"-thick bone-in pork chops

1 Preheat air fryer to 400°F.

2 Combine oil with spices in a small bowl until well mixed.

3 Pat pork chops dry with a paper towel and evenly rub oil mixture on all sides.

4 Place pork chops into ungreased basket of air fryer and cook 6 minutes.

5 Flip pork chops and cook 5 more minutes.

6 Transfer cooked pork chops to a cutting board, let rest 5 minutes, then serve.

PER SERVING
Calories: 364 | Fat: 22g | Sodium: 674mg |
Carbohydrates: 1g | Fiber: 0g | Sugar: 0g |
Protein: 35g

Slow Cooker Italian Sausage with Peppers and Onions

SERVES 6

Put your slow cooker to use while you are out, and come home to a wonderful dinner ready to feed the whole family. Portion any leftovers in individual containers for future meals throughout the week or freeze for later. Serve over pasta, alongside rice, over cauliflower rice, on a crusty baguette as a sandwich, or over shredded green cabbage for crunch.

PREP TIME: 10 MINUTES ● ACTIVE COOK TIME: N/A ● HANDS-OFF COOK TIME: 6 HOURS

1 (28-ounce) can unsalted crushed tomatoes, including juice

¼ cup water

1 tablespoon kosher salt

1 tablespoon Italian seasoning

¼ teaspoon crushed red pepper flakes

6 cloves garlic, peeled and crushed

2 pounds uncooked mild Italian sausage links (about 8 links)

2 large yellow onions, peeled and thinly sliced

2 large green bell peppers, seeds and ribs removed, sliced into ¼"-long strips

1 bay leaf

1 In a 5-quart or larger slow cooker, combine tomatoes, water, spices, and garlic.

2 Add sausage links, onions, and peppers. Toss to combine, making sure sausage links are mostly submerged.

3 Tuck bay leaf into sauce, set slow cooker to high for 6 hours. If you have the option, set cooker to warm when cooking time is done until ready to serve.

PER SERVING
Calories: 607 | Fat: 45g | Sodium: 2,288mg | Carbohydrates: 19g | Fiber: 5g | Sugar: 8g | Protein: 25g

Tips, Substitutions, Time-Savers, and More
Serve topped with chopped parsley, crushed red pepper flakes, and a bit of grated Parmesan. To add some heat, try substituting spicy Italian sausage or using half mild sausage and half hot sausage.

CHAPTER EIGHT

EFFORTLESS SWEET TREATS

You know that feeling when you are desperately craving a sweet treat and want something more than a handful of chocolate chips or a spoonful of peanut butter? In this chapter, you will find effortless sweet treats that only take a few minutes to make—and don't make a huge mess.

Feel like s'mores but don't want to deal with starting a fire or individually roasting marshmallows? Take all of the work out of it by whipping up a Baked S'mores Dip with Graham Crackers. Or pop a healthy whole-food 5-Ingredient Chocolate Freezer Fudge into the freezer, and, after it's set, cut a piece and indulge in that chocolate craving. Or use fiber-rich apples as a base for 4-Ingredient Apple Nachos. You can have this delicious sweet treat ready to enjoy during your favorite show before the commercial break is over! Keep your pantry stocked with the easy-to-find ingredients in Appendix A to make effortless sweet treats your new reality.

Maple Vanilla Microwave Mug Cake

SERVES
1

Combine a handful of pantry staples to create the ultimate easy single-serving dessert in under 5 minutes from start to finish. Serve right in the mug!

PREP TIME: 2 MINUTES ● ACTIVE COOK TIME: N/A ● HANDS-OFF COOK TIME: 2 MINUTES

2 tablespoons salted butter
2 tablespoons pure maple syrup
2 tablespoons whole milk
1 teaspoon pure vanilla extract
¼ cup all-purpose flour

1 Place butter in a microwave-safe mug (at least 12 ounces). Place in the microwave and melt on medium power for 20–30 seconds.

2 Add maple syrup, milk, and vanilla. Use a small whisk or fork to beat until smooth.

3 Add flour and continue whisking until flour is completely dissolved.

4 Microwave for 1½–2 minutes, starting with 1½ minutes and checking to see if it is done before continuing with additional cook time. (The range of cook time allows for variability in microwave power, size, and brand.) Allow to cool for 1 minute before serving with a spoon.

PER SERVING
Calories: 450 | Fat: 22g | Sodium: 198mg | Carbohydrates: 53g | Fiber: 1g | Sugar: 26g | Protein: 4g

Tips, Substitutions, Time-Savers, and More
Serve topped with a dollop of whipped cream or peanut butter, chocolate chips, sprinkles, or even a scoop of your favorite ice cream. Substitute the whole milk for any plain, unsweetened milk of your choice.

Baked S'mores Dip with Graham Crackers

SERVES
8

Craving s'mores but want an easier version with much less cleanup? This s'mores dip is ready in 10 minutes, including baking time. Customize by using your favorite type of chocolate chips, like milk, semisweet, dark, or white chocolate chips. Both mini and jumbo marshmallows work great. You can also double or even triple the recipe for a crowd.

PREP TIME: 2 MINUTES ● ACTIVE COOK TIME: N/A ● HANDS-OFF COOK TIME: 8 MINUTES

½ tablespoon salted butter

1 (10-ounce) bag milk chocolate chips

1 (10-ounce) bag mini marshmallows

16 2-cracker graham cracker sheets, halved

1 Preheat oven to 450°F.

2 Spread butter on bottom and sides of a 9" cast iron skillet or similar-sized oven-safe baking dish. Pour in chocolate chips and top with marshmallows.

3 Bake 8 minutes.

4 Remove from oven to a heat-safe surface and cool 5 minutes before serving. Once dip has cooled, use graham crackers to scoop up dip.

PER SERVING
Calories: 428 | Fat: 13g | Sodium: 190mg |
Carbohydrates: 72g | Fiber: 2g | Sugar: 46g |
Protein: 5g

Campfire-Style Baked Banana Boats

SERVES 1

Baked banana boats are an easy and healthy sweet treat that take almost no time to prepare. Customize with your favorite nut butter and chocolate combo, and you have a truly effortless dessert.

PREP TIME: 3 MINUTES • ACTIVE COOK TIME: N/A • HANDS-OFF COOK TIME: 15 MINUTES

1 medium-sized ripe banana

1 teaspoon creamy unsweetened peanut butter

1 teaspoon milk chocolate chips

1/8 teaspoon flake salt

1. Preheat oven to 350°F.

2. Leaving the skin on, slice banana 3/4 of the way lengthwise through the center from top to bottom.

3. Gently push sliced banana apart and spread peanut butter along inside of banana. Sprinkle chocolate chips on top of peanut butter and finish with salt.

4. Wrap banana in tinfoil and place on a baking sheet. Bake for 12–15 minutes or until warmed through. Serve immediately.

PER SERVING
Calories: 155 | Fat: 4g | Sodium: 313mg |
Carbohydrates: 31g | Fiber: 4g | Sugar: 17g |
Protein: 3g

Tips, Substitutions, Time-Savers, and More

Substitute any type of nut or seed butter you have on hand. Same for the chocolate chips: dark chocolate, white chocolate, a broken-up chocolate bar—all will work! The banana skin will turn black when baked—this is okay.

178 • The "I Don't Want to Cook" Book

4-Ingredient Apple Nachos

SERVES
2

These 4-Ingredient Apple Nachos are perfect whenever you have a sweet craving, are short on time, and still want something made with good-for-you ingredients. Some tasty additions, if you have them on hand, are toasted coconut flakes, granola, chopped walnut or pecan pieces, or chopped Medjool date pieces.

PREP TIME: 5 MINS ● ACTIVE COOK TIME: N/A ● HANDS-OFF COOK TIME: 30 SECONDS

2 medium Gala apples, cored, seeded, and sliced

2 tablespoons creamy unsweetened peanut butter

1 tablespoon pure maple syrup

2 tablespoons milk chocolate chips

1 Arrange sliced apples on a serving dish.

2 In a small bowl, combine peanut butter and maple syrup. Microwave for 30 seconds and stir until well combined.

3 Drizzle nut butter mixture over sliced apples and top with chocolate chips. Serve immediately.

Tips, Substitutions, Time-Savers, and More

Don't have Gala apples? No problem: Use any in-season apple that is tasty enough to eat raw.

PER SERVING
Calories: 280 | Fat: 11g | Sodium: 10mg | Carbohydrates: 38g | Fiber: 5g | Sugar: 30g | Protein: 5g

One Bowl Peanut Butter Blondies with Chocolate Chips

MAKES 16 BLONDIES

This incredible peanut butter–based dessert is so quick and easy—just dump all of the pantry-staple ingredients into a large bowl, mix, pour the batter into a baking dish, and bake. These store and freeze great and can be tucked away for future desserts. For extra flavor, sprinkle a pinch or two of flake salt over the top before baking!

PREP TIME: 10 MINUTES • ACTIVE COOK TIME: N/A • HANDS-OFF COOK TIME: 22 MINUTES

1 large egg
1/2 cup creamy unsweetened peanut butter
1/4 cup salted butter, melted
2/3 cup granulated sugar
1 tablespoon pure vanilla extract
1 1/4 cups all-purpose flour
1 teaspoon baking soda
1/4 teaspoon kosher salt
4 ounces semisweet chocolate chips, divided

1 Preheat oven to 350°F. Line an 8" × 8" oven-safe baking dish with parchment paper.

2 In a large mixing bowl, combine egg, peanut butter, melted butter, sugar, and vanilla. Add in flour, baking soda, and salt. Mix until well combined.

3 Fold 3 ounces chocolate chips into dough. Press dough into prepared baking dish in an even layer.

4 Sprinkle remaining 1 ounce chocolate chips onto dough. Press down gently so that chips are mostly in the dough.

5 Bake on center rack 20–22 minutes until light golden brown.

6 Remove and allow to cool completely in baking dish, about 1 hour. Once cool, cut into sixteen squares. Serve or store covered at room temperature up to 2 days, in refrigerator up to 1 week, or in freezer up to 3 months.

Tips, Substitutions, Time-Savers, and More

Chunky peanut butter can be substituted for creamy for more texture. Coconut sugar can be swapped for granulated sugar. For a gluten-free version, substitute 1 cup blanched almond flour plus 1/4 cup cassava flour for the all-purpose flour and bake for 20 minutes.

PER SERVING
Calories: 183 | Fat: 9g | Sodium: 143mg | Carbohydrates: 21g | Fiber: 1g | Sugar: 13g | Protein: 4g

Dump and Bake Peanut Butter Cookies

MAKES
24
COOKIES

Dump and Bake Peanut Butter Cookies combine five easy-to-find pantry ingredients to make a delicious and easy homemade cookie in a little over 20 minutes. For peanut butter chocolate chip cookies, fold ½ cup of chocolate chips into the dough.

PREP TIME: 6 MINUTES ● ACTIVE COOK TIME: N/A ● HANDS-OFF COOK TIME: 15 MINUTES

1 cup creamy unsweetened peanut butter, room temperature

1 large egg

¾ cup granulated sugar

1 teaspoon baking soda

¼ teaspoon sea salt

1 Preheat oven to 350°F. Line two baking sheets with parchment paper.

2 In a medium bowl, combine peanut butter, egg, sugar, baking soda, and salt until well mixed.

3 Measure a tablespoon of dough and roll into a ball, making a total of twenty-four little balls.

4 Use a fork to press each dough ball down onto prepared baking sheet.

5 Make an additional fork press on each cookie in the opposite direction so that the two-fork presses form a cross.

6 Bake for 14–15 minutes.

7 Allow cookies to rest on baking sheet for 2 minutes, then transfer to a wire cooling rack. Cool completely before storing.

Tips, Substitutions, Time-Savers, and More

Allow the peanut butter and egg to get to room temperature before using. To make a peanut butter and jelly thumbprint cookie, skip the fork indents and use your thumb to press a well into each cookie. Fill each well with a small amount of your favorite jam or jelly and follow the same baking instructions.

PER SERVING
Calories: 93 | Fat: 6g | Sodium: 71mg | Carbohydrates: 8g | Fiber: 1g | Sugar: 7g | Protein: 3g

Sweet and Salty Chocolate Bark

SERVES
8

Create homemade chocolate bark in minutes using your microwave to quickly melt a bag of milk chocolate chips. Add salted roasted peanuts, pretzel pieces, and a hint of flake salt for a Sweet and Salty Chocolate Bark that will make a delicious sweet treat for weeks to come.

PREP TIME: 10 MINUTES • ACTIVE COOK TIME: $2\frac{1}{2}$ MINUTES • HANDS-OFF COOK TIME: N/A

1 (10-ounce) bag milk chocolate chips

$\frac{1}{2}$ teaspoon coconut oil

$\frac{1}{2}$ cup salted roasted peanuts

$\frac{1}{2}$ cup salted mini pretzels, broken into pieces

2 teaspoons flake salt

1 Line a baking sheet with parchment paper.

2 Place chocolate chips and oil in a large microwave-safe bowl. Microwave on high $2\frac{1}{2}$ minutes, stirring every 30 seconds, until chocolate is smooth and completely melted.

3 Pour melted chocolate onto prepared baking sheet and use a spatula to evenly spread out so the melted chocolate takes up about 75 percent of the baking sheet.

4 Working quickly so the chocolate doesn't set, evenly sprinkle peanuts, pretzel pieces, and salt over chocolate. Transfer baking sheet to freezer for 2 hours to set.

5 Break into pieces and store in a covered container in the refrigerator up to 1 month.

PER SERVING
Calories: 274 | Fat: 14g | Sodium: 739mg | Carbohydrates: 29g | Fiber: 2g | Sugar: 19g | Protein: 6g

Watermelon "Pizza" with Whipped Cream and Fresh Berries

SERVES 8

This fun and colorful fruit-based dessert uses rounds of watermelon as a "pizza" base ready to decorate with whipped cream and fresh berries. Just slice the finished rounds into "pizza slices," serve, and watch it disappear!

PREP TIME: 15 MINUTES ● ACTIVE COOK TIME: N/A ● HANDS-OFF COOK TIME: N/A

1 medium-sized ripe watermelon, cut into four 1"-thick rounds through the center

1 cup whipped cream

1 quart fresh blueberries

1 quart fresh strawberries, hulled and thinly sliced

1/2 cup unsweetened flake coconut

1 Line two baking sheets with parchment paper.

2 Place two watermelon rounds on each baking sheet, and gently pat the top of each round with paper towels.

3 Spread 1/4 cup of whipped cream on each watermelon round in a thin layer. Decorate whipped cream with blueberries and strawberries. Sprinkle each round evenly with coconut.

4 Refrigerate 15–30 minutes until topping is set. Remove, slice each round into 6" slices, and serve immediately.

PER SERVING
Calories: 289 | Fat: 5g | Sodium: 7mg | Carbohydrates: 62g | Fiber: 7g | Sugar: 47g | Protein: 5g

Tips, Substitutions, Time-Savers, and More
You can substitute any in-season berries or even pitted cherries for the blueberries and strawberries.

Pecan Brownie Dessert Smoothie

This decadent smoothie is a single-serving dessert you don't need to feel guilty about. It tastes like a pecan brownie but is made with only whole-food ingredients that are easy to find. Try adding a dollop of whipped cream on top. Any type of plain, unsweetened milk can be substituted for the almond milk.

PREP TIME: 3 MINUTES • ACTIVE COOK TIME: N/A • HANDS-OFF COOK TIME: N/A

1 cup plain, unsweetened almond milk

½ teaspoon pure vanilla extract

1 tablespoon unsweetened cocoa powder

1 tablespoon pure maple syrup

1 large Medjool date, pitted

2 tablespoons pecans

1 small ripe banana

8 ice cubes

Add all ingredients to a blender. Blend until smooth and creamy. Serve immediately.

PER SERVING
Calories: 349 | Fat: 13g | Sodium: 184mg | Carbohydrates: 62g | Fiber: 9g | Sugar: 42g | Protein: 5g

5-Minute Whipped Chocolate Mousse

SERVES
4

Use your stand mixer or hand mixer to make decadent chocolate mousse in 5 minutes. Make sure to sift the cocoa powder and powdered sugar for the smoothest texture. If you prefer a dark chocolate flavor, increase cocoa powder to 4 tablespoons and reduce the powdered sugar to ¼ cup. This can be made up to 24 hours in advance. Excellent served with whipped cream on top.

PREP TIME: 5 MINUTES ● ACTIVE COOK TIME: N/A ● HANDS-OFF COOK TIME: N/A

1 cup heavy whipping cream

½ teaspoon pure vanilla extract

3 tablespoons unsweetened cocoa powder, sifted

⅓ cup confectioner's sugar, sifted

1 Chill a large stainless steel bowl or the bowl of a stand mixer 15 minutes.

2 Once chilled, add cream and vanilla. Whip on medium speed 2 minutes.

3 Add cocoa powder and sugar, and whip 3 more minutes until fluffy and peaks start to form.

4 Cover and refrigerate up to 3 days until ready to serve.

PER SERVING
Calories: 248 | Fat: 21g | Sodium: 23mg | Carbohydrates: 12g | Fiber: 2g | Sugar: 10g | Protein: 2g

Tips, Substitutions, Time-Savers, and More
What is sifting? Sifting is when you pour your dry powdered ingredients like flour, powdered sugar, cocoa powder, or baking soda over a fine mesh strainer or sieve to break up any clumps and to aerate the powder. This results in a smoother batter, as the sifted powder will be more finely incorporated.

Caramelized Bananas with Greek Yogurt and Walnuts

SERVES
1

This simplified version of caramelized bananas is an indulgent treat ready in under 5 minutes. While it's excellent paired with plain Greek yogurt and walnut pieces, you can also use it as a topping for pancakes, waffles, or your favorite ice cream.

PREP TIME: 2 MINUTES ● ACTIVE COOK TIME: 2 MINUTES ● HANDS-OFF COOK TIME: N/A

1 tablespoon salted butter

2 teaspoons granulated sugar

1 large banana, peeled and cut into $1/4$" rounds

$1/2$ cup full-fat plain Greek yogurt

2 tablespoons walnut halves

1 Heat a 12" skillet over medium-high heat. Once hot, add butter. Once melted, about 30 seconds, sprinkle sugar over butter and shake skillet to mix.

2 Place banana pieces directly on top of sugar mixture and sauté 1 minute, shaking skillet frequently. Flip banana pieces and sauté 1 more minute.

3 Remove and serve over yogurt, topped with walnuts.

PER SERVING
Calories: 445 | Fat: 24g | Sodium: 132mg | Carbohydrates: 46g | Fiber: 4g | Sugar: 30g | Protein: 14g

5-Ingredient Chocolate Freezer Fudge

Spend 5 minutes making this rich and silky chocolate fudge and keep it stashed in your freezer for any time a chocolate craving hits. For a nutty twist, add ½ teaspoon of almond extract to the batter.

PREP TIME: 5 MINUTES • ACTIVE COOK TIME: N/A • HANDS-OFF COOK TIME: N/A

1 cup refined coconut oil, melted
1 cup unsweetened cocoa powder
⅔ cup pure maple syrup
1 teaspoon pure vanilla extract
¼ teaspoon kosher salt

1 Line an 11" × 7" baking dish with parchment paper.

2 Add all ingredients to a blender. Blend 1½–2 minutes until fully incorporated.

3 Pour batter into prepared baking dish and place in freezer for at least 1 hour, up to 3 hours. Cut into sixty-four squares before serving.

PER SERVING
Calories: 82 | Fat: 7g | Sodium: 19mg | Carbohydrates: 6g | Fiber: 1g | Sugar: 4g | Protein: 1g

Tips, Substitutions, Time-Savers, and More

Refined coconut oil is not the same as virgin coconut oil. Virgin coconut oil has that signature "coconutty taste" and can be substituted as long as you are okay with a strong coconut flavor.

APPENDIX A:

PANTRY STAPLES

Having a well-stocked pantry is critical when it comes to whipping up flavorful, healthy meals in no time. The items listed here are the core pantry staples you'll want to have on hand to make many of the recipes in this book as well as other easy dishes. All these items are shelf-stable (meaning they are packaged to be stored at room temperature for a long time) and widely available at most grocery stores. These are the ingredients you will grab repeatedly as you effortlessly create dishes like Pressure Cooker Pulled Pork (Chapter 7), Black Bean Sheet Pan Nachos (Chapter 6), and Creamy Paprika Chicken Skillet with Spinach and Tomatoes (Chapter 7).

When it comes to cooking oils, the recipes in this book focus on three main types: olive oil for medium-heat cooking, chilled foods, salads, and marinades; avocado oil for high-heat cooking (because of its high smoke point of over 500°F, and because it is neutral in flavor and has a mild taste); and toasted sesame oil for adding that deep, nutty, complex flavor in Asian-inspired dishes.

The dried herbs and spices in this list are crucial for adding blasts of flavor when you don't have fresh herbs on hand. You will find that many of the recipes in this book rely on dried herbs and spices to make it easier for you and to avoid any unnecessary grocery store runs. Consider buying these dried herbs and spices in bulk: They are not only much cheaper but are also usually a lot fresher.

- Nonstick Cooking Spray
- Avocado Oil
- Extra-Virgin Olive Oil
- Balsamic Vinegar
- Red Wine Vinegar
- Apple Cider Vinegar
- Rice Vinegar
- Toasted Sesame Oil
- Tamari (or Soy Sauce or Coconut Aminos)
- Fermented Fish Sauce (like Red Boat brand)
- Olive Oil or Avocado Oil Mayonnaise
- Organic Sugar or Coconut Sugar
- Arrowroot Starch or Cornstarch
- Canned Beans (Black Beans, Pinto Beans, Kidney Beans, White Beans, Garbanzo Beans)
- Unsalted Diced Tomatoes
- Unsalted Crushed Tomatoes
- Unsalted Canned Tomato Sauce
- Enchilada Sauce
- Pickled Jalapeños
- Yellow Onions
- Whole Heads of Garlic
- Canned Unsalted Dolphin-Safe Tuna
- Canned Wild Alaskan Salmon (No Skin or Bones)
- Pizza Sauce

- Frank's RedHot Original Cayenne Pepper Sauce
- Sriracha
- Yellow Mustard
- Dijon Mustard
- Pickled Jalapeños
- Roasted Red Peppers in Water
- Pitted Kalamata Olives
- Sliced Kalamata Olives
- 24-Ounce Jars Marinara Sauce
- Low-Sodium Chicken Broth
- Low-Sodium Vegetable Broth
- Long-Grain White Rice
- Pasta (Fusilli, Bow Tie, Orecchiette, Uncooked Lasagna Noodles, Orzo)
- Couscous
- Red Lentils
- Brown Lentils
- Steel-Cut Oats
- Pure Maple Syrup
- Pure Vanilla Extract
- Local Raw Honey

- Unsweetened Cocoa Powder
- Unsweetened Natural-Style Peanut Butter
- Plain, Unsweetened Nondairy Milk of Choice (Almond, Rice, Soy, Coconut, Oat)
- Chocolate Chips (Milk, Dark, White, or Semisweet)
- Hearty Tortilla Chips
- Sliced Almonds
- Whole Walnuts (or Halves and Pieces)
- Kosher Salt
- Flake Salt
- Ground Black Pepper
- Black Peppercorns
- Dried Bay Leaves
- Ground Cumin
- Turmeric
- Dried Thyme
- Old Bay Seasoning
- Chili Powder

- Curry Powder
- Dried Parsley
- Taco Seasoning
- Everything Bagel Seasoning
- Paprika
- Smoked Paprika
- Crushed Red Pepper Flakes
- Italian Seasoning
- Dried Dill
- Garlic Powder
- Ground Cinnamon
- Ground Ginger
- Ground White Pepper

APPENDIX B:
SAMPLE SHOPPING LIST

When it comes to making delicious, easy recipes in minutes, there are a few fresh grocery items you will want to have on hand. The items listed here represent the most commonly used ingredients across the recipes in this book. Use this list to plan your trips to the store.

Another way you can save time and effort is to look for already prepped versions of frequently used ingredients like onions and garlic. Many stores sell chopped or diced onions in the refrigerated convenience vegetables section. Keep in mind, however, that jarred, minced garlic does not have the best flavor. Instead, look in the convenience vegetables section for bags or containers of peeled garlic cloves. Since most of the recipes in this book call for crushed garlic, all you need is a few peeled cloves and a garlic press.

For the fresh gingerroot in this list, buy a large piece and stash it in a freezer-safe bag in your freezer. When you are ready to use it, grab a microplane and grate the frozen ginger (skin included) into a small dish.

When it comes to dairy products, you will always get the best flavor, texture, and performance from full-fat dairy. Low-fat dairy products usually have stabilizers or gums added to them and can often taste chalky or watery.

And the freezer is the best place for fresh bread. Use high-quality freezer-safe bags to store sliced bread, bagels, muffins, tortillas, and rolls to make delicious sandwiches, wraps, tacos, and quesadillas in minutes.

To Stock the Refrigerator:

- Eggs
- Salted Butter
- Cream Cheese
- Shredded Mozzarella Cheese
- Shredded Mexican-Style Cheese
- Greek Feta Cheese
- Grated Parmesan Cheese
- Heavy Cream
- Basil Pesto
- Hummus
- Wild Alaskan Smoked Salmon
- Shredded Green Cabbage
- Shredded Carrots
- Fresh Baby Spinach
- Spring Mix
- Rotisserie Chicken

To Stock the Freezer:

- Gingerroot
- Frozen Peas
- Cooked White or Brown Rice for Reheating
- Frozen Sweet Corn Kernels
- Frozen Corn on the Cob
- Frozen Chopped Spinach
- Frozen Vegetable Mix for Stir-Fries
- Individual Portions Wild Alaskan Salmon Fillets (About 6 Ounces Each)
- Uncooked Peeled and Deveined Medium to Large Shrimp
- Rotisserie Chicken Meat (Cubed or Shredded)
- Ground Turkey
- Ground Beef
- Ground Pork
- Bulk Italian Sausage
- Mild or Hot Italian Sausage Links
- Chicken Wing Pieces
- Boneless Skinless Chicken Thighs
- Boneless Skinless Chicken Breasts
- 1"-Thick Bone-In Pork Chops
- 1"-Thick Boneless Pork Chops
- Thick-Cut Bacon
- Sliced Bagels
- Sliced English Muffins
- Sliced Sourdough Bread
- Sliced Jewish Rye Bread
- Long Baguettes
- 9" Flour Tortillas
- 100% (5") Corn Tortillas

US/METRIC CONVERSION CHART

OVEN TEMPERATURE CONVERSIONS	
Degrees Fahrenheit	Degrees Celsius
200 degrees F	95 degrees C
250 degrees F	120 degrees C
275 degrees F	135 degrees C
300 degrees F	150 degrees C
325 degrees F	160 degrees C
350 degrees F	180 degrees C
375 degrees F	190 degrees C
400 degrees F	205 degrees C
425 degrees F	220 degrees C
450 degrees F	230 degrees C

BAKING PAN SIZES	
American	Metric
8 × 1½ inch round baking pan	20 × 4 cm cake tin
9 × 1½ inch round baking pan	23 × 3.5 cm cake tin
11 × 7 × 1½ inch baking pan	28 × 18 × 4 cm baking tin
13 × 9 × 2 inch baking pan	30 × 20 × 5 cm baking tin
2 quart rectangular baking dish	30 × 20 × 3 cm baking tin
15 × 10 × 2 inch baking pan	30 × 25 × 2 cm baking tin (Swiss roll tin)
9 inch pie plate	22 × 4 or 23 × 4 cm pie plate
7 or 8 inch springform pan	18 or 20 cm springform or loose bottom cake tin
9 × 5 × 3 inch loaf pan	23 × 13 × 7 cm or 2 lb narrow loaf or pate tin
1½ quart casserole	1.5 liter casserole
2 quart casserole	2 liter casserole

WEIGHT CONVERSIONS

US Weight Measure	Metric Equivalent
1/2 ounce	15 grams
1 ounce	30 grams
2 ounces	60 grams
3 ounces	85 grams
1/4 pound (4 ounces)	115 grams
1/2 pound (8 ounces)	225 grams
3/4 pound (12 ounces)	340 grams
1 pound (16 ounces)	454 grams

VOLUME CONVERSIONS

US Volume Measure	Metric Equivalent
1/8 teaspoon	0.5 milliliter
1/4 teaspoon	1 milliliter
1/2 teaspoon	2 milliliters
1 teaspoon	5 milliliters
1/2 tablespoon	7 milliliters
1 tablespoon (3 teaspoons)	15 milliliters
2 tablespoons (1 fluid ounce)	30 milliliters
1/4 cup (4 tablespoons)	60 milliliters
1/3 cup	90 milliliters
1/2 cup (4 fluid ounces)	125 milliliters
2/3 cup	160 milliliters
3/4 cup (6 fluid ounces)	180 milliliters
1 cup (16 tablespoons)	250 milliliters
1 pint (2 cups)	500 milliliters
1 quart (4 cups)	1 liter (about)

INDEX

ABOUT THE AUTHOR

Alyssa Brantley is the creator of the popular recipe website EverydayMaven
.com, where she shares seasonal recipes built on real-food ingredients. Her
motto is "Whole Food. Half the Time." Alyssa deeply believes that just
because we are busy doesn't mean we shouldn't eat great! In addition to
sharing her kitchen creations, Alyssa is a food writer, food photographer, and
food stylist.

Alyssa was raised in Philadelphia and now resides in Seattle with her
husband and two sons. Having grown up in a cooking family, Alyssa learned
to love food and to explore flavors, cuisines, and ingredients from a very
young age.

While living in New York City for college, Alyssa was an intern at the
Food Network. During graduate school, she started a successful corporate
lunch catering business called Grub Catering. *EverydayMaven* was started
after the birth of her first son, when she was looking for a creative outlet and
began sharing the recipes she was using to lose extra pregnancy weight.

When Alyssa is not getting creative in the kitchen, she loves to travel,
especially exploring new cities by walking and eating, spending time with
her family, reading, and drinking wine on a sandy beach.

Her recipes and food photography have been featured by Today.com,
HuffPost, *Real Simple*, *Clean Eating*, *Gourmet*, *Shape*, *Self*, *Prevention*, *Parade*,
Redbook, *BuzzFeed*, and more.

ACKNOWLEDGMENTS

Thank you to my husband, Kareem, who made me believe in soul mates, long hugs, and sitting quietly, and for giving me the gift of finally knowing what it is like to be with someone who loves and accepts you 100 percent for exactly who you are. I love you more than I ever knew was possible.

To my children, Deacon and Vaughn, the loves of my life and my forever taste-testers. Watching you both learn to love new foods and explore diverse types of cuisine is a true joy. Thank you for giving me honest feedback, loving flavor, and giving me the gift of a love I did not know was possible.

To my parents, who have always loved good food and wine. For never thinking we were too young to take to a five-star restaurant. For encouraging us to try all the things, all the time, for not giving us basic kid food. For normalizing driving three hours (or more!) for a great meal, seeking out the best restaurants and chefs, and teaching us what it means to genuinely love food and explore other cultures' cuisines. And, for always loving me as hard as possible, regardless of the circumstances.

To my brother, Adam, the real chef in the family, who has a sixth sense for flavor combining and seeking out the best food anywhere in the world. One of the most generous, selfless humans I've ever known—and maybe the most sarcastic.

To all of my family and friends old and new. And especially for the friendships that fill my soul and give me life. Those who have always been there: Mike, Jen A., Jen B. (formerly known as Jen W.), Jenna L., Jen B., Megan A., Traci, Drea, Farrah, and, last but in no way least, Tina.

To all of my website readers and followers who inspire me every day. Thank you for challenging me to try new ideas and new cooking techniques, and giving me a reason to share new recipes with the world.

To my culinary mentors and inspirations. First and foremost, my mom. Everyone at the original Food Network, especially David Rosengarten, Bobby Flay, Emeril Lagasse, and, of course, Julia Child.

To the food writing, food photography, and food blogging communities for continuing to level up the game and raise the bar. Food has never looked so good.

And to everyone at Simon & Schuster and Adams Media for making this project happen and turning pandemic cooking burnout into something fun and delicious.

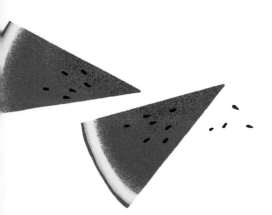